THE WORKINGS OF
THE SUBTLE HEART

The Workings
of the
Subtle Heart

William Widmer

Alacrity
BOOKS

Designed and composed in Fournier MT at Hobblebush Books, Brookline, New Hampshire (www.hobblebush.com)

Printed in the United States of America

First Edition

Publisher's Cataloging-In-Publication Data
(Prepared by The Donohue Group, Inc.)

Widmer, William.
   The workings of the subtle heart / William Widmer.

   p. ; cm.

   Includes bibliographical references.
   ISBN-13: 978-0-9797562-0-7
   ISBN-10: 0-9797562-0-0

   1. Religion and poetry. 2. Mysticism and poetry. 3. Spiritual life. 4. Poetry--History and criticism. I. Title.

PN1077 .W53 2007
809/.93382

Published by:

ALACRITY BOOKS, INC.
P.O. Box 1168
Amherst, New Hampshire 03031

For Eckhart Tolle, who inspired me to write this book, and for Kurt Vonnegut, who inspired me to write.

Contents

Chapter 1 · Facing God

Chapter 2 · Rough-and-Tumble

Chapter 3 · Mind-Poise

Chapter 4 · The Flow of Sanctity

Chapter 5 · Spiritual Vanity

Chapter 6 · Dimensions of Guidance

Chapter 7 · Fare Forward, Travelers!

Preface

THERE IS A WAY OF KNOWING, in fine detail, that proceeds from the heart.

This knowing is as subtle as the subtlest thoughts of some so-very-bright, stratospheric physicist, for example;

but rather is a subtle knowing that is achieved in the domain of feeling.

Have you ever watched a famous violinist, some dusty old master, near the end of his career, play the violin? His face contorted under some finely articulated inner rapture, which is now generating music through him?

That's the kind of thing I mean.

THE WORKINGS OF
THE SUBTLE HEART

❖❖ 1 ❖❖

Facing God

✳ Peering into the Mist

WHEN I WAS A BOY of maybe ten or eleven, my parents and
brother and I went up north to our summer vacation at a cabin
on a remote lake, an hour's journey from the last major road-
way. Through deep woods wound spidery, overgrown, wandering roads, paved to unpaved, which suddenly opened before us,
coming at last to the glint of sunlight upon water. And then still
miles along the water before we reached the cabin, a darkly angled
building hung on a low ridge near the lake, in an inlet, a kludge of
rough lumber and nails, with a misshapen, low outside table and
a path to the dock. The next morning, I woke up first, and I went
outside early. It had gotten colder overnight, and the cabin and the
lake were all fogged in. One could almost drink the fog.

I went outside like a nearly blind person, hands before me, seeing
only a foot or two before me badly in the mist, and made my way
barefoot alone to the dock, the water nearly invisible but for its
slap against the small pilings, and walked the gray boards of the
dock to the very end. And stood there, on the water, in the fog,
and listened.

"Listened for what?"

And watched.

"For what? Watched what?"

But upon an electric edge I realized that I was not alone there! And
I ran back to the cabin, across the weathered gray docks, across
sand, across the stones, the pursed weeds . . . my feet, somehow,
knowing all they touched.

ﯾﺐ

✳ Penetrating Poetry

AS A TEENAGER, I wrote poetry, as do many teenagers, forced or otherwise.

Usually, it's forced. Although a surprising number of people have tried to write poetry with some level of seriousness, prior to giving it up. And yes, just about all give it up (by the way) weighted down by the deadening effects of the practical world and the coarsening effects of age.

There are a few years between childhood and adulthood in which poetry has any significance at all. Almost no adults read poetry, really.

Poetry frustrates those people who have a strong need to make clear sense out of everything, which is most people; and all those uncomfortable with ambiguity avoid it. The attainment of its intangible rewards are hard to obtain; occupying, as it does, a domain that cannot be rendered into straight sense, and so must be found via another sense, or found not at all.

Like anything of significance, it takes a fair amount of energy to penetrate poetry.

People generally accept that it takes a considerable amount of work to understand, say, calculus. But poetry? Either they think they like a certain poem, or they think they don't like it. Few people ask themselves if they have actually mastered it, in any objective way.

So poetry has always been, and remains, a marginal sort of activity and interest that engages but the few. For good or ill, it is of significance only to those who get *that* particular thing, this poetry.

Anyway, as a teenager, I wrote poems, and I would go out into the countryside and "be poetical."

What this meant, in practice, was that I would go to some remote spot, and would clear my mind and be fully there; and upon its own moment, would sense something. That *something* was always an explicit something. A specific taste. Not a vaporous thing at all.

❋ The World Is Not a Collection of Things

BY WAY OF EXAMPLE, you might imagine that it is early winter, in a land of farms and deep forests, way up north; and having grown housebound, you have pulled on your old trail-boots and gloves, and made your escape into the sharper cool.

And that you have now made the short way across your backyard, and across the fence and overgrown field that trails up to the old farm up the hill; and there have entered the woods, first guided on an old path and then by the remembrance of years, as you hike that way up. The sky is gray and rolling and smelling of snow.

The earth is frozen in some spots, and still soft underfoot in others, and there is the smell of earth and wood, bracken and stone. The interwoven branches, twisted fingers of the naked trees above you motion upward; the black-green pine, beyond, in broader and finer gesture.

You encounter an old dirt road, disused and tending toward weed, which you take up and which leads to the top of a large hill.

The road up is hemmed in by the woods. No one will go up or down this road until the springtime.

As you walk up the hill, you rise above the common level of the trees, the wind freshening from the north. The sky is so gray, it almost seems a shade of purple.

And up ahead, a low ledge approaches the road from both sides until one is in a gently sloping valley, a small V still forested among a facing of rock. To one side, from a fractured face of gray-black rock, you notice a small trace of water. And approaching, you see the steady flow of this water down the angular face, framed by ice, and below the trees, ferns still and mosses beaten-green outlining where the earth and water slip away downhill. A little pool, before running into the woven undergrowth. And the gray only deepens.

And then, out of nowhere, a sense of imminence . . . the gathering of something, or the quick reduction of something, like the house lights being dimmed;

and then, in a shudder, a burst: everywhere snow, snow everywhere, a dance of flakes twirling silently through the naked trees. The sky white now in silent spiral.

Swirling white!

And then you realize that you are the only person for mile upon mile; and that all you can hear is the little water spilling down the rock, so quiet that you can even hear each flake coming to rest on your shoulder, between the oscillations of your own breath.

And then you enter a sudden, profound, quiet space; as you realize that this little piece of the world is not a collection of things, but is rather the Face of a fuller spirit, a Face that now spots its own delightful reflection in the mirrors of your eyes. A Face across which transcendent emotion plays, as fluidly as the swirl of flakes is carried by the vagaries of the wind.

Seeing Itself in you, now.

❋ Fullness & Distraction

THAT'S WHAT I USED TO call being poetical. Stuff like that.

Am I writing well enough for you to understand what I mean?
Are you the right kind of reader to understand what I mean?

A sense of Fullness in a sense of Place.

* * *

Perhaps in the example that I just gave, that place amidst the early
snow would have been less compelling at a different time of year,
or with company other than oneself.

Or, perhaps it would have been less compelling under the same
circumstances, alone in the snow, if one had been worried about
a sick child, or had sore feet, or wondered where one would get
money to get the car fixed.

Or, I suppose . . . whether one could find one's way back in the
gathering snow.

There's an endless source of distractions; some real, some less so.

But maybe, just maybe, if you were there in the right frame of
mind, in spring during bud-break, there would be a magic there,
too. Or perhaps in the hum of the August heat. A different magic,
perhaps. A different fullness.

Many, many people understand this fullness, whether they call
it fullness, or peace, or do not give it a name at all. It's nearly
impossible to be a farmer, for example, and not sometimes know
the fullness of your land. Those trout fishermen in the small and
rocky waters are there for more than the fish. And it is no accident

that certain golfers awaken upon dreaming of the view across a particular fourth hole, in a May twilight, as they follow their ball in flight.

People are there for more than the exercise, the harvest, the score.

Something is singing to them there.

Now, the point I wish to make before getting on with the rest of my story is that this fullness that is sensed by the farmer, or the fisherman, or the golfer is the same fullness that is sensed by the poet. It is the same fullness sensed by the mystic. There is only one Fullness, the experience of which is modulated only by the manner of entry and the depth of one's surrender to It.

✺ Fullness Demands Poetry

BUT LET'S LOOK at poetry by itself for a moment.

It is of course no secret that the sacred texts of all people are either full of poetry or entirely poetry. What are the Psalms but poems? What is the gospel of John but one long poem?

In the beginning was the Word

and the Word was with God

and the Word was God.

The Qur'an? The Tao Te Ching? The Bhagavad Gita? Poetry, poetry, poetry.

A certain Fullness demands poetry, and at the age of seventeen, I sought to be a poet.

I was, in some sense, on a collision course with Fullness.

❊ A Catching of the Flavor

AT SEVENTEEN, I was a self-declared agnostic.

I was raised a Catholic, and an ardent one. My agnosticism, in retrospect, was pretty short-lived. But like many other teenagers, I had decided to put aside my beliefs, and then to think about them and add them back in one at a time, as they seemed true to me.

Poetry was true to me.

I liked taking long walks in the deep country, as far away from people as I could get. I'm not a real social person, it seems. I like being alone.

I always have. Always will.

I grew up on the edge of the country, and during my walks, if the fields and forests around me struck me in a particular way, I would stop, and fully attend to *this place*, and often would absorb a moment of particular peace. In this peace was a presence felt, and as I would pull away from it, I would feel an exquisite something. A knowing of something. A catching of the flavor of something.

I know this probably sounds kind of bizarre, but it's kind of like a sudden strong sense of smell, which resolves itself somehow to knowledge. A taste, as it were.

One spring afternoon, after school, I drove my parents' car into the countryside, twenty miles from home, on a rural road through farm fields. I had gotten my license only a month or two earlier, and taking the car for a ride was still, well, kind of a kick. This was a time of the small family farm, and there were many farms in various stages of upkeep along the main road and the many dirt side roads. It was a cool April day, and the sky was rolling gray.

Being late April in the North, the buds were just coming out red on the old maple trees along the roads amid stone walls built by farmers long dead.

I pulled up one side road, past the little farm on the corner, and drove a half-mile down the road and parked the car on the shoulder, next to a pasture that was so very green green.

The open land rolled upward for another half mile before a little hill, and as I got out of the car, I noticed that the wind was up.

As I walked up the hill, the wind pushed me from behind.

The smell of spring filled the air: earth and grass, cow and water.

I followed the meandering road gently uphill. The land below rolled to a low spot flanked by rising fields, and then spread again, out to the distant farm downhill.

Uphill, across the broad stone walls, the fields rippled slowly like a sea stopped, as it made its way across the brow of a small hill, gesturing away.

The road moved up a natural cleft in the land; and to the right, a dozen old maples ascended the road in a line. The fields were bordered by old stone field walls, which meandered along with the road.

The red branches of the maples danced in the wind.

As I approached the top of the little hill, it started to rain lightly—a very light, windblown rain, up from behind me.

I decided to go back to the car. I braced for heading back into the wind, and as I turned back and looked over the narrow rise that I had just ascended, I came upon . . . the most beautiful thing I had ever seen.

It was just the green fields, rolling away to the distant farm; the stone walls running downhill; the wind in my face; the red branches of the old maples responding perfectly to the wind. And I stood there and just emptied myself.

I had such great joy. It was an almost sexual joy, like looking in a lover's eyes.

And then, I somehow recognized something remembered in this landscape; something out of time that was now, yes, somehow again.

And as I looked at the scene before me, my joy, inexplicably, continued to rise. It was an accelerating joy that was no longer *my* joy, but rose of its own accord, under its own guidance, and it began to pull me out of myself. I became subordinate to *it*.

As the joy in me rose . . . accelerated . . . a flow, then a torrent, ran through me, upward, striking like a series of notes, and I quickly changed.

In a moment, the energy rose to my throat, and I suddenly grew larger than my body; I was able to look at the exterior surfaces of my body from all around, from each angle, from many distances, at the same instant. I looked deeply into my own eyes, at the back of my own head, without ever losing the sense that I had one, unified perspective.

No longer bound by my body, my unified senses were independent of my body and capable of understanding the essence of things by their interpenetration.

I was no longer bound by the apparent surfaces of things, but knew them in their interpenetration: trees stone air earth. I heard the stone recite *IamIamIamI IamIamIamI IamIamIamI IamIamIamI,* and the sound was like the sound of stone on stone.

And as I sought to discern how stone could have such a presence, I caught sight of God, the movement of water upon water, who delighted, laughing. Emerged as the Reality of the *I am* of the stone. Unimaginably ancient, alive in incomprehensible fullness. And He laughed me.

We laughed together! Like a mirror I was to Him, like a Mirror He to me!

And was then directed to the making of the world; witnessed as the Most Real created all that we experience at a particular moment: the instant creation of the substance of the world by His ongoing will. What we experience, at *any* moment, exists at the instant will of God.

Wake Up!

What we experience, at *this* moment, exists at the instant will of God.

And yet my self turned again to only God.

And I was a simple thing, light upon light, in the light of God. And yet I was delimited; my light had an edge, when laid upon the light of God. And in that bliss there was no span, no duration; no before or after.

(In some fundamental way, whatever it was that I was, before, went away then; and has never returned.)

Emerging from the light, I was with God, in unlimited joy, being allowed to participate in the nature of things. My God! God makes the universe as we make love!

But better! Better!

And then, in the sweep of such joy, I was aware of my body standing on the roadside, and then I felt . . . saw a certain energy being coiled into my nature, and then, and then . . .

I found myself standing along the road, laughing in the wind and rain.

* * *

I've told you now, a little, about what happened that April day. But as you might expect, I cannot describe fully what occurred. Words cannot capture it. The mechanical limits of my human mind cannot process it.

It's beyond report.

But it's still there, right there.

Still there.

❀ A World Hidden

IN THE MONTHS that followed this event, while I was still seventeen, I wrote two poems.

Here's one of them.

> There is a world hidden men
> freight around beyond the corners
> of their eyes, ungraspable
> in the black
> Smiling out its blackness crookedly
> on canvas paper air
> it is most unknown most
> untouchable most unattainable best
> loved   Struggling to free
> itself to nothingness beyond
> the dice roll to the place
> where ice boils—where space
> is inscrutable and the stars
> closed mouth

✳ Contemplation Is Everywhere

JUST ABOUT ALL of the major religions have a branch, or branches, whose primary practice emphasizes contemplation.

Christianity, for example, has within the Catholic and Orthodox churches a great tradition of contemplative, monastic orders— the Trappists, the Benedictines, the Franciscans, the Hesychastic monks of the Orthodox Church; and many others, whose numbers now dwindle. And there are still a few persons who pursue solitary lives as religious hermits.

Buddhism is a philosophy singularly organized toward, and vivified by, contemplation.

Hinduism has yoga fulminating at its core, and the aphorisms of Patanjali, written in the second century B.C., have never been rivaled in the depth of their understanding of contemplative practice. The Indian culture was the first to develop a high understanding of mind-poise.

The vision-quest of the American Indian is a journey of contemplation.

The Sufis have distilled the inner aspects of Islam into a contemplative mysticism of immense depth.

I could go on and on.

And so as exotic, and perhaps, to some ears, as foreign, as all these orientations may sound, this contemplation of which I speak is indeed everywhere.

In farmers and fishermen and teenage kids, and lovers looking into each other's eyes.

✳

❀ Organ of Spiritual Perception

THE SUFIS HAVE A CONCEPT, that in order for someone to be fully spiritually awake, a specific organ of spiritual perception needs to be opened.

Once it is opened, that understanding which was missed is now perceived. The Sufis understand this capacity to be affiliated with the opening of the *Lataif*, which is translated as *The Subtleties.*

The Subtleties are a capacity, like seeing; while the organ of spiritual perception, the heart, is like the eye.

You can't see unless your eyes are open and working; but if your eye does work, you can take in a huge amount of knowing in but a glance. The sky, mountain, lake and lodge before you.

When one's heart is open, one may take in a large spiritual understanding in a similar glance.

* * *

Let me give an analogy for what I mean.

I am told that there is a Japanese word, *sabishii*, that is commonly translated as "melancholy"—but the Japanese word does not carry, exactly, the same connotation as that English word.

How can one translate the untranslatable?

Well, you might imagine yourself as Japanese (if you are not Japanese), a Japanese of a hundred years ago, who is standing on the promontory overlooking a bay, as twilight descends.

A few minutes ago, you might imagine, you just said goodbye to someone you love very much, a hard moment followed by that person boarding a sailing ship, which is just now raising its sails as it begins to make its way out of port.

The ship suddenly picks up speed and you can see the sails now in full billow.

And then you stand on a rise on the shore, watching the progress of the ship as it heads out to sea, watching it as it slowly makes its way to the horizon; rapidly at first, and then resolving itself, slowly, to an ever smaller dot . . .

And then . . . *sabishii* is that very moment when you lose sight of the ship.

A distillation, as it were, of the gathering and scattering of intertwined lives, hopes, fears, and dreams, crystallized into a thing of no size and no duration. Which hangs out of time, in meaning.

To perceive this inclusively, in a single moment, is like the operation of the organ of spiritual perception of which I speak.

And once recognized, it can be trained, a little.

Do you recognize it?

✤ Ramakrishna

THE NINETEENTH-CENTURY Hindu saint Ramakrishna Paramahamsa, as a child, fell into an ecstatic state after watching a flock of white cranes take to the sky.

Let me ask you: What was it that caused Ramakrishna to fall into a state of ecstatic vision? The white cranes?

The operation of the organ of spiritual perception involves the receipt of something, in the same way that hearing is the receipt of sound, or seeing is the receipt of light.

Just as the eye must be open to see, the heart must be open to spiritually perceive. In some sense, it was Ramakrishna's heart that flattened him, a heart in relation to the cranes; which (by the way) are more than "just cranes."

As William Blake says: "Ev'ry bird that cuts the airy way is an immense world of delight, closed by your senses five."

The operation of this mode of spiritual perception requires a certain contemplative alignment. It requires something like mindfulness—an attentiveness that is not dispersed by chattering thought or untoward emotions; an attentiveness that is even more focused than simple mindfulness. An attentiveness that is more anticipatory, which expects more of the *now*. An alignment whereby all dullness of heart is cast off, where the heart may dance like a leaf in the breeze. Where something like the rising of a flock of white cranes, from the green fields to the blue sky, a-squawk with their rising, may knock one down with the sheer joy of it all.

✻ Contemplative Alignment

AT THE OUTSET of this experience of mine, I was standing along a road, in the wind and rain, looking down on rolling green fields, rolling away to the distant farm, the stone walls running down-hill, the wind in my face, the sweep of the maple branches in the wind.

The process began, I think, because I was able to gather and direct my full attention, my full being, all my senses, my full will, an open heart, a focused mind toward One Thing, at one instance, in contemplation. It was an *alignment process*. Or better, a process that *aligned*.

It was the first time in my life that all elements of my being were in alignment, and this alignment was created by my self opening to something greater, which was beyond myself, in the immediate now.

Over the past thirty years, all subsequent spiritual experience has shared these common elements; a certain contemplative alignment of all aspects of my being, in the now.

✳ Secrets

IT MUST BE TIME for a poem:

> There are just some secrets
> demand telling that can't be.
>
> Too fleet for words, step
> beyond my words, are not
> made of words. Inhabit the
> spaces between my words.
> Whistle at me whilst
> in transit. There.
>
> That rock pointing there.
> That rolling cloud past
> the October sun.

✻ Sacred Time

AND UPON THIS rapid convergence of all aspects of my being, this coming into alignment, the first sense was that I had recognized something remembered in this landscape, something out of time, which was now, again. That I had entered sacred time.

I had experienced this sacred time before, of course, as has almost all of humanity; but at perhaps a lesser volume.

As a kid raised Catholic, I had this same sense of sacredness on Good Friday afternoon. On Easter morning.

A sense that *this* was the day that Christ died, that *this* was the day that Christ rose.

Not as some day of simple commemoration, but rather as a day when past, eternal events poked forward into the now. A day made holy by the cycle becoming coincident with a past event that was somehow out of time.

And what I sensed, standing on that low green hill, was like a sudden realization that I had forgotten that it was Easter morning. A sudden recollection of something of great importance. A waking up into something of great moment, of great joy.

✳ Arising in Joy

AT THIS SENSE of discovered glory, my joy turned to wonder, and my wonder turned to joy, and impossibly, my joy continued to increase, until it was no longer *my* joy, but was rather a large and expanding thing to which *I* belonged. Concurrently with this overflow of joy, I felt a strong arising, as though I was in a column of wind that was blowing from the ground, straight up, but through me without resistance.

I was suddenly aware of some sort of connection at the base of my spine, which was instantly drawing into me some force that pervaded the countryside around me, which my expanding joy drew up around me in a rush.

And as my joy expanded, and as there was this upward rush, I felt myself vibrate, accelerate, at an impossible progression. In the wake of this acceleration, a note like some metaphysical gong struck at mid-body, and I accelerated to it. A moment later, it sounded at upper-chest and bounced to that resonance, and a moment later . . .

I found myself as a sentient cloud, surrounding my body to a significant distance, looking at the back of my head, looking into my own eyes.

✴ The Sexual Aspects of Enlightenment

THERE WAS, to be frank, an aspect of the sexual in this arising.

Many spiritual people get squeamish when there is any hint of the intersection of spirituality and sexuality. As a Catholic, I must observe that my church has turned such squeamishness into an art form; which has leaked out of the church in a spate of recent scandal.

* * *

Putting aside this squeamishness, let me discuss the energetics of sex.

If one is in a situation that one finds arousing, there is a clear awareness of a certain flow of sexual energy in that arousal.

When one becomes aroused, one can feel a certain energy flowing into the sexual regions.

If one turns away, for a moment, from one's sexual interest and toward the changes that are happening very quickly in the body, it will be found to have as its origin a place in the spine, partway between the navel and the tailbone.

Now let us say that the evening has progressed and one is engaging in sexual congress. As relations continue, a greater and greater degree of energy is built up in the sexual regions, and upon orgasm, that energy is released upward, to the brain. Note this the next time you have an orgasm. One's awareness is instantly converted from the sexual regions to be focused within the head, at the moment of orgasm.

Speaking energetically, one develops a significant and highly responsive energy in the lower part of one's being, which ultimately, upon orgasm, rings first a bell in one's sexual organs and lower spine, and then, in turn, a bell in one's brain.

My point is that there was a similar but more dramatic upward movement of energy during my experience.

As the joy in me grew at a geometric rate, I recognized that something was happening—that the joy was an energy from outside me, flowing into me from a great distance, and then was translated upward.

It was like a series of notes being struck as the energy rushed upward. And my being changed in a series of fixed steps. I was accelerated.

This is about the best description that I can muster of what happened, energetically, but I am also aware of how *exotic* it all sounds when described this way. Although there were aspects of this energetic transformation that I had not experienced before and have not experienced since, there were other aspects that were, as I have mentioned, in some sense quite familiar.

✺ Connections to the Larger Universe

WHEN I STOOD THERE on that spring day and poised my vision upon the green horizon, my attention found a place of rest amid the sweep of the land, and the joy that arose in me, and flowed out of me, created, in some sense, a *pull*. When this pull occurred, I was suddenly aware of having energy being drawn into me from a distance. It was something like discovering that I was unexpectedly waist-deep in water, which was somehow being drawn into me at the base of my spine and flowing upward, upward and outward.

So it is no surprise to me that the image of a fountain is a recurrent symbol in many spiritual writings. For the arising was like a fountain, but far less tame. It was a viscerally radical experience, like going from standing still to going, say, to a thousand miles an hour in just a few seconds.

I accelerated as it hit my solar plexus with an inner sound as if a note had been struck, and accelerated again as it flashed at mid-chest, with a geometrically higher note being struck, and again at the throat, and then, and then . . .

✸ Spiritual Transitions

NOW, I AM NEITHER a physicist nor a mathematician, but in retrospect, it is abundantly clear to me that the progression which I experienced was an inherently mathematical progression of sorts. Further, it was a discontinuous progression, in that it started at one value and continued to absorb energy in that state until the energy was adequate to cause another state change, to a far higher, but somehow logical, value. Sometimes analogies are helpful, and sometimes misleading, but the process seemed similar to how atoms reportedly change frequency states when excited.

The next thing I experienced was being removed from my body and looking at the exterior of myself from many angles at once, including looking into my own eyes.

✺ A Wilderness Shelter

LOOKING INTO my own eyes.

Into the interior of my own hazel eyes, their pupils wide in the green expanse, and also at the back of my head, and also at my whole body from all directions, from above and below, near and far away, from right and left. And my eyes, my eyes . . .

Too bad my eyes will go away when I die.

But after all, my eyes are just an accommodation to this world, like a makeshift wilderness shelter is an accommodation to a coming storm, something abandoned upon the rising of the new morning. Abandoned in the journey forward.

As T. S. Eliot says in *Four Quartets,* "Not fare well / But fare forward, voyagers."

My eyes, for one thing, shall not fare well. Too bad, too bad . . . but forward I go.

✺

✳ Excellence Requires Multiple Points of View

I SUPPOSE THE GOOD NEWS is that there is a unified perceptual state that is beyond vision and is not dependent on the physical organ of the eye.

One obvious meaning of my ability to look into my own eyes, and at the back of my own head, is simply that I was no longer dependent on my physical eyes, but was independent of them and my body.

One human mental habit that this experience destroyed was the mental habit of one point of view. I had no fixed locus. I had no front or back. I had no up or down. I was both near and far from my body. And within that perceptual state, which had no reference to distance from the body, or the cardinal points of the compass, or orientation to the effects of gravity, I had great freedom in my point of view. Was liberated, as it were.

Excellence in all matters requires multiple points of view, in some manner of simultaneity. This is a point worth noting.

❋ A Unified Perceptual State

MY PERCEPTION, at this point, was a "unified perceptual state," a term which sounds almost legalistic. So what exactly do I mean by this?

Well, let me start to explain this by first quoting the poet and mystic William Blake:

"For man has closed himself up, till he sees all things thro' narrow chinks of his cavern."

I think that the narrow chinks to which Blake refers are the five physical senses. What one commonly understands as one's sensory input through the five senses is still there when one's sensing is whole, in the same manner that what is perceived of the sky through the narrow chinks of a cavern is still there, were one to leave the cavern.

It's simply that the gaps which made the perception partial have now been filled in.

During my experience, hearing was part of the continuum of seeing. And was bridged, by something, to seeing.

Tasting was part of the continuum of hearing. And was bridged, by something, to hearing.

Seeing was not bound by apparent surfaces, but the knowing heart proceeded through Reality as it willed. Perception as an unbroken circle.

This is not some rarefied version of what we now experience.

It is what we now experience, and much, much more. Not esoteric. Not stranger.

More, more. Just much more.

As Blake says:

For the cherub with his flaming sword is hereby commanded to leave his guard at the tree of life, and when he does, the whole creation will be consumed and appear infinite and holy, whereas it now appears finite & corrupt.

This will come to pass by an improvement of sensual enjoyment.

The gaps between the chinks are filled in by this sensual improvement. Through the discussion of sensuality, Blake makes of himself a stumbling block, but if one surmounts this challenge, one has life in abundance. The fullness of the providence of God.

Our birthright as God's children is greater capacity of the senses, not less.

✴ The Mystic Peers Through the World

AFTER FINDING MYSELF looking into my own eyes, I "heard" something. What I heard was *I am I, am I am I.* And the voice was of stone.

I know this must seem odd. But what I discovered, in that disembodied state, was that the universe is *declarative.*

In our normal, embodied state, we perceive things through bits of sensory information and put them together in a way so as to make sense of them, to determine what they are, and what is going on.

In this new state, things declare what they are. This unified perception, this unified knowing, has only to choose what it attends to, and that thing is instantly and fully opened to it.

The voice of stone was not like the voice of a person, but of stone reciting its own nature.

It was voice as a force of nature. It was a voice that was like the embodiment of a physical principal, the operation of a law. And the physical principal vocalized was simple, sheer being. That it was. And moreover, that it was stone.

Imagine stone being rubbed against stone. The sound of stone on stone was the quality of its voice. A voice heard, felt, seen, known.

* * *

Rumi says:

> *Because the idol is your face,*
> *I have become an idolater.*

Rumi understands Who is under the Idol of the World.

Animism or idolatry, though less excellent than a full understanding of God, senses something of God within His creation. It is this inward recognition that is enough for Rumi to declare himself one of their party.

For while we know God above the world, it is partly through the world that we know God . . .

The mystic does not become disentangled from the world, but rather learns to peer through its features.

❀ It's Because It Is

THE REASON the mystic can find God in the *now* of the world of experience is that whatever *is* derives its being from God; and as such has a certain metaphysical saliency.

Because of that, *that* which *is* deserves a certain manner of respect.

The inanimate objects around us are not self-reflective. Nonetheless, these objects are more substantial than we usually understand them to be, since they derive their existence by the instant will of God.

☀ The Nature of God

EARLIER I WROTE:

And as I sought to discern how stone could have such a presence, I caught sight of God, the movement of water upon water, who delighted, laughing. Emerged as the Reality of the I am, of the stone. Unimaginably ancient, alive in incomprehensible fullness. And He laughed me.

We laughed together! Like a mirror I was to Him, like a Mirror He to me!

In a momentary questioning of the *I Am* of the stone, I caught sight of God, who, being caught, emerged in delight, as a parent might reveal himself or herself in a game of hide-and-seek to a young child.

Strange as that must sound.

The attributes of God were declarative. The attributes of God, being of God, were themselves discernible Being.

God was Person.

Not an embodied person. But then again, I suppose, neither was I.

God was a God of staggering antiquity; which I know must sound strange.

In Daniel, God is called "the Ancient of Days." If you have ever been to one of the medieval cathedrals of Europe, you may understand what I mean when I say that "age hangs upon them."

But that sense is but the barest whiff of the antiquity that hangs upon the Ancient of Days.

Strange as this may sound.

Delight. Joy. What delight God takes in His own Nature!

Mercy. Compassion! How good He was to me, and continues to be!

✳ Our Relationship with God

AND YET He was also like a mirror to me—someone whom I was part of, someone who, in some sense, was part of me. I was like a four-year-old, who had just awakened to the sunlight, having all night feared those two big bumps near the end of her bed, only to discover her feet!

We laughed!

I was kindred in nature to God. We were of the same stuff, but not the same person.

We are, in fact, God's children.

This is not a metaphorical expression.

But we are not God.

✳

✳ The Making of the World

AND THEN, as if answering an implicit question about how the world was made, I was shown in slow motion, as one might be shown how a magic trick is done.

And again, God's attributes were declarative.

The world was made by a simple act of God's will, and what an iron will it is!

Absolute. Uncontested. Incontrovertible.

The making of the world was a simple act, a snap of the fingers. And yes, an act, *His* act. The universe was not a universe on autopilot. The universe has God's intention to it. The world is an aspect of God's intention.

The world is a simple act of God's will. *Now* is a simple act of God's will.

You experience Him here, now, if you could but realize it.

✳

✸ Six Words

I HAVE LABORED for many years to find an appropriate expression of what the world is to God. At great length, I have found the appropriate six words:

The world is God's sock puppet.

It is not an illusion, nor is it completely real.

And God makes it sing and dance without mouth or feet.

✌

✳ A Simple Thing

AND FROM THAT, I became . . . light.

I was a simple thing, light upon light, in the light of God.

White-yellow light, the same color and intensity as the sun, in an endless sea of light.

I was unaware of the existence of time, had no sense of before or after. Just being in ecstatic joy, light upon light.

But, oh my light had an edge; as thin as a human hair, set upon an overall sea of light.

I was overlaid, light upon a greater Light.

* * *

I am reminded of a poem by Rumi, translated by Coleman Barks, about an Islamic dervish, or holy man:

Someone said, "there is no dervish, or if there is a dervish,
that dervish is not there."

Look at a candle flame in the bright noon sunlight.
If you put cotton next to it, the cotton will burn,
but its light has become completely mixed
with the sun.

That candlelight you can't find   is what is left of a dervish.

Oh, I was light upon light, and time was no more.

It is this aspect of the experience to which I have given the most thought over the past thirty years, this aspect that has given me my greatest joy, and my greatest suffering.

Then:

Emerging from the light, I was with God, in unlimited joy, being allowed to participate in the nature of things. My God! God makes the universe as we make love! But better! Better!

Time moved again, and I had a role in the nature of things—in great joy, having great fun. Close to God, who was also having great fun.

Fun.

Is it strange to think of God having fun?

All good things bound into that Fun!

※

❦ A Return to the World

AND THEN IN THE SWEEP of such joy, I was aware of my body standing on the roadside, and then I felt . . . saw a certain energy being coiled into my nature, and then, and then . . .

I found myself standing along the road, laughing in the wind and rain.

I became aware of my body in the midst of a broad field of regard, and being conscious of my body as my center of regard, I was twisted in a quick spiral back into my body, as a spring is wound in a grandfather clock. And I saw a certain energy wound into myself as part of the process.

And upon that winding, I knew that what had happened to me was not over, but would be further revealed in that unwinding of that coiled gift. And it is the unwinding of that energy, over the past thirty years, that I would like to now tell you about.

* * *

(My God, is it really more than thirty years ago that all that happened?)

It seems like just yesterday, really.

I suppose it is this disconnect that ultimately causes the elderly to finally come to grips with Eternity. That thirty years ago seems, really, just like yesterday. It exposes apparent time for the fiction it is. Simply what went before, and not in any sense long ago, at all, at all.

Thirty years ago, I was not yet married, had had no kids, had not spent twenty-five years as a middle-manager at the same large corporation. I had no house. No arch supports. No reading-glasses.

My die had not yet been cast.

Or perhaps I just did not know it.

⊷ 2 ⊷

Rough-and-Tumble

✳ The Power of Miracles

I HAVE TOLD the story of my effacement in God to only a small number of people over the past thirty years.

One reason I have told it so seldom is that in the few instances when I have told it, the story has usually been wildly misunderstood, and people have almost immediately taken a position on its merits or lack thereof.

For example, people who more or less believed what I told them asked me if, because I was allowed to participate in the nature of things, and know God, and understand the break point from which miracles are made, could I then (you know) perform miracles?

It must be known that God accords *only* those *few* people who can be trusted with such, the ability to perform miracles.

God knows that should my heart have the sudden power of miracles, that half of my neighbors for half a mile around would be suddenly afflicted with freak accidents and fulminating diseases, as would the great preponderance of their pets.

Both God and me think that it's best not to allow me to touch the levers of Reality anytime soon.

❦ Yankee Spirituality

LIVING, AS I DO, in New England, I see in this desire to somehow blast half of one's neighbors to the root, a certain Yankee spirituality.

The spirituality of the mill owner.

The spirituality of the boardinghouse spinster. Of the farmer with gout.

And is an advanced spirituality not so much for what it gives itself over to, but moreover to what it restrains itself from giving itself over to.

A Yankee forbearance of action.

A forbearance of satisfying the root drive that has roiled the Middle East for the past six days, six months, sixty years, six hundred years . . . indeed, for the past six thousand years, blow upon blow upon blow. Whereupon the record ends.

* * *

Or, at least we don't satisfy it *here,* mostly.

❦

✸ Difficulties in Sharing Ultimate Experiences

AFTER MY EXPERIENCE, some of the first few people I told were my teenage friends. Their invariable reaction was, "Man what (drugs) were you doin'? You must have been sooo freakin' high."

'Fraid not. Unless one considers poetry a drug.

Only marginally better was the later response from a variety of upright, rational, demonstrably smart people, who would start to analyze my experience—usually in the form of perceptive comments about old brain/new brain electrical imbalances, or perceptive theories generated on the spot about chemical or biological processes, pathological psychology, and, at least on one occasion, a Freudian interpretation by one charming old man who had studied psychology, in college, in 1938.

It would be fair to say that my story was not an unalloyed success. Then again, I suppose that I was not telling it particularly well, either.

Then there were, as I have mentioned, those people who *more* than believed what I told them. And thought that I was now due a tremendous elevation in their opinion, and showed me *awe*.

My God, save me from awe! It was the worst reaction of all, for its sheer insidiousness.

Of the twenty-some odd people to whom I have told this story, perhaps eight of them quickly found their own mental explanation that debunked, in some manner, the experience. They assumed that it was some sort of pathology, further explored it to see whether that pathology was still operant or was definably episodic.

I could watch them shift gears, considering the possibility that I was now, or formerly had been "mental."

Now, these were not twenty people chosen at random. Rather, they were people I had hoped would take something from this conversation, people in whom I had recognized a special something, people I had hoped would somehow make this a *special* conversation.

So. These were twenty-some odd people chosen over thirty years. Chosen with trepidation. One every year or two.

Of those twenty-something, eight bailed out quickly. Two others were awestruck, tremulous when I appeared in a doorway.

Several others took my story in stride. They assessed it as an experience among experiences, as another story that generated a few status points. They could not see that the story was outside the dimensions of the typical story, in that the person telling it had, in some sense, not survived the experience.

As for the rest, several of them, though more reflective, more willing to allow my report of the experience to sprawl amorphously before them, had their objections.

There were those with theological objections of one sort or another.

The overly Christian was dismayed that my experience did not contain imagery that was more fully redolent of the Book of Revelation. Was disappointed that I did not recount seeing the throne of God, the streets toward which are paved with carnelian & gold.

And upon that disappointment, suspect.

The Buddhist did not approve of my finding God as a Person, abstract Person though He may be. Believed that it was not, in some sense, *politically correct* to make such a discovery.

Strangest of all was the one who took my story in stride, prompted me along in its orderly recitation, asked no substantive questions, and just allowed me to talk. He thanked me for *sharing* my story, and never mentioned it again. God knows what he really thought, if he thought anything at all beyond the human relations of the telling.

Much of what I have learned in thirty years about human beings' involvement with spiritual matters, my own and others', has come from reflection on such reactions.

* * *

Then thankfully, there were the three people who knew exactly what I was talking about.

For of those twenty-odd persons, over that thirty years, I had chosen well. Those three!

ﺟﺐ

✺ Those Three!

HOW CAN I DESCRIBE the meeting with those three?

Well, imagine, if you will, an old married couple that is obliged to go to some tedious dinner party, where both suspect that the hostess will drink too much, just as she did last time. And who will stand up near the end of dinner and begin to ramble on about some passionate cause in which she is a true believer, just as last time.

And imagine that old married couple, sitting across the table from each other, looking at each other from between the candles & flowers, in the midst of the predicted speech. And as that hostess pauses her oratory for a sip of wine, the wife looks at her husband, a bare trace of a smile on her lips, and winks—a perfect wink, causing in both a perfect inner laugh, hidden from everyone but each other. That exquisite laugh!

With those three, it was all winks and laughs, and figures traced in the air!

Oh, yes, we indeed knew well.

ﭘ

✳ Aftershocks

THE DAY AFTER, and the week after, and the month after my experience of God, I was still in shock. Profound shock.

Not exultation? (I have, remember, told this story twenty-some times.)

No. Shock. Shock.

And why?

Because the experience, in some intense way, refused to go away. Refused to go away. Refused to become part of history.

As T. S. Eliot says in *Four Quartets,* "That which is out of time / is available to all time."

A smart man, Mr. Eliot, and an excellent mystic. For the experience, being in an existential sense out of time, was now coexistent with time, and refused to go away. But why was that a problem?

How may I explain?

❋ A Comfortable God

MOST PEOPLE, if and when they have a sense of God, or an image of God, have such an image or sense on a fleeting basis, and at other times go about their business; go about the leading of their lives. The notion of God that they have is, in some sense, a comfortably remote sense; a God of another dimension, a God as a philosophical construct.

Mother Earth as God, the Universe as God. God as Idea. Something to reflect on in the odd moment of this harried life.

Whereas I, as a seventeen-year-old, had seen God as the source of my entire experience, moment by moment. And not only was He, in some sense, a full part of all that I had experienced, but His nature was in me as experiencer as well.

He was now fully latent in all, unavoidably shining through it like the sun.

Prior to the experience, I used to like to lie on the sofa and watch, say, *Gilligan's Island* reruns; and then to try to figure out the series of moves that would allow me to get my hand up Missy's sweater that evening.

It was a pretty big change.

❋ God Is Always There

AFTER ABOUT A MONTH, I realized that I had not been truly unconscious since the experience. During the day, I was alarmingly aware of the presence of God, and at night, at night . . .

Well, imagine that you are on a beach in the summer, in the early afternoon, and you fall asleep while lying in the sun, in a beach chair on the sand.

Even while you are asleep, you are still aware that the sun is beating down.

My sleep was like that, pervaded even in the absence of dream by the presence of God. Shining, shining, shining, shining.

There was no being out. There was no being away. He was there always, always.

✳ The Ego as Banal

MUCH OF WHAT I HAD ENJOYED before the experience was revealed to be incredibly banal. And though banal, I still felt the destitution of these things as a loss.

The loss of desire for the hot car. The loss of desire for fame and adventure. Banal losses, but losses nonetheless, in that crescent of things lost as part of that finding. But there was that finding!

The world, now, was color-saturate.

There was still the lingering sense that my very being, in some way, interpenetrated the things of the world. A sense of being intuitively excellent. Intuition as a competency, as tangible as wiggling my fingers.

Unfortunately, this intuition led to a sense of loss . . . in people.

* * *

People were not a very pleasant experience for me in the months that followed my effacement in God.

Now, how can I talk about this and make any sense at all?

Well, did you ever know someone well, and sometime later meet his or her father, and realize that the person had his or her father's laugh? Raised his eyebrows in surprise the same way? Had the same hand gesture when making key points?

That although you now had more knowledge about that person, the person was in some sense less of an individual now, because aspects that you believed were part of his or her individuality were revealed to be part of his father's patrimony? Simply the result of passing habits down through the generations?

In the months following my experience, I experienced people as agglomerations of inherited and socialized traits that lay over them like a crust, punctuated by moments of light, by the actions of a real person.

Those true moments were rare in some people and seemed nonexistent in others. And all this conferred the knowledge of the personality as banal. More obstacle than vehicle.

That revelation was the hardest of all.

❋ Every Niggling Evil

IN THE MONTHS FOLLOWING my effacement in God, the sheer banality of human society was like a hot poker driven inside me.

At that time, and in other times since, I have had the ability to discern, in a direct, forcible, and immediate manner, the nature and quality of people's souls. Of their existential wholeness—or, far more usually, of their lack of existential wholeness. Fragmented parts of mutually irreconcilable personalities, held together like pieces of armor duct-taped over the sensitive thing underneath. Absorbed in a conventional game of the giving and receiving of status, the giving and taking of offense, the instant risings and passings of sexual desires, fantasies of power or money, plans for food, need to urinate. A constant judgment of everyone encountered, based on a large spectrum of biases: the well dressed against the less well dressed, the better dressed against the merely well dressed, the tall against the short, the old against the young, the bright against the unbright; the unkind against the kind, the less prosperous against the more. People entwined in an incredibly complicated net of envy and disdain.

And I could immediately see in myself all that I saw in others. That there was no sin of which my heart was incapable. But was instead virtuoso in every niggling evil.

Now, thirty years later, I am more upbeat than all that.

But back then, I had an increasing sense of having to hold myself together in the face of all that I had seen and was then seeing. The constancy of God, the banality of evil in human society of which I was a part.

And then, after several months of increasing tension, my personality broke down.

I despaired. My despair was complete.

✱ Demons

IT MUST BE TIME for a poem:

> "Oh, the human being
> every each and every
> of us, every each,
> has one or more demons.
> One or more.
>
> More often. Don't
> be ashamed.
> It's OK.
>
> That giving over.
> That weight."

✸ The Breakdown of Personality

THERE WAS NO STATE I could imagine that was authentic, other than in the obliteration into God, which I now feared. I was sunk in despair, my own dark night of the soul, and in this despair, the dialogue in my head just stopped.

Just about all of what we call the personality is maintained by an internal dialogue. The personality is the atmosphere created by our internal dialogue. When our internal dialogue stops, so does our personality, in some fundamental way.

Within, there was just dark silence. This was not a silence that required effort to maintain, but rather a silence that could be broken only by the gravest efforts to think.

Dark Silence unopposed.

Now, the personality leads one to believe that if one were to try to do without it, one would wind up like a catatonic in a mental ward, with spittle running down one's chin.

Whereas, in fact, one lives and interacts just fine without a personality.

Without a personality, one does what one needs to do, says what one needs to say, bears without question the responsibilities dictated by the inward situation. Acts in an excellent manner, without cunning. Without preplanning. Without self-interest. Lives in a fluid space, and when met with demands, meets those demands based on a response from the dark ocean, with a certain ineffable grace.

Now, thirty years later, when my thinking falls away, as it sometimes does for months at a time, I rejoice in a certain sense of grace and freedom. A certain wholeness for which I give thanks to God!

But still I must confess, those many years ago, when my thinking first went away, I tried to think, believing that one needed to think to be. I was anxious that I was not thinking, had to try consciously to think, to calm myself over not thinking.

Like a child sometimes grabs on to a chair while learning to walk, I was learning to live without it, sometimes.

✸ A Rough-and-Tumble Thing

SO. I GOT PRETTY WELL whacked around over the course of those first few months.

Based on the experience of those months, and over the past thirty years, my notion of what it is to grow in the spirit is inseparable from getting whacked around.

Let me say it again: There is no growth apart from getting whacked around.

Any and all spiritual benefits that may accrue to you will cost you something.

Any of them.

All new growth will cost you a piece of your old self, and I'm afraid that it may be a piece that you're not completely done with yet.

Just ask Jesus crucified. You're never quite ready for anything that counts. *Eloi, Eloi, lama sabachthani?*

A rough-and-tumble thing is this growth in spirit. Not for the faint of heart.

✹ Prophet Stuff

IT MUST BE TIME for a poem.

As I have written, I believe that the ability to endure a certain existential pain is a prerequisite to spiritual growth.

There is a strain of over-commercialized, feel-good spiritual trea-
tises now making the best-seller lists that suggest that God will
give one leave not only to grow rich and have all manner of good
things on earth, but also to be unequivocally saved in the world
that is to come. The gain-without-pain approach.

Let me call now on the spirit of Jeremiah, and the spirit of Christ
crucified, and respond:

> "Popular always are the preachers
>   who say that the love of God will compound
>   your blessings. That health, wealth, fame,
>   love . . . are the fruits of His love,
>   as though love of Him were
>
>   a voodoo ritual. Oh, write
>   your love for Him upon a scrap of paper, used
>   by an old black woman, and burn it
>   early morning following a
>   full moon!
>
>   Ye idolaters!
>
>   For He offers nothing but Himself.
>   Requires no fine wrappings. Obviates
>   lesser needs. he that provides the lesser
>   is not Him.
>
>   Be warned."

❋ Infinitely More Aware

THIS PROPHET STUFF is pretty cool.

* * *

But where was I? (Oh, yeah,) age seventeen-plus, a few months after my experience, and I had broken down a bit under its weight, and yet I also was very much alive in a certain force-of-nature way.

I was very, very awake.

Earlier, I mentioned that in these first months, the presence of God was full and consuming. That God was the undercurrent of day, the undercurrent of night.

That my daily consciousness bobbed around dramatically.

It seemed to me that I had a hole in my nature, an upward well of sorts that existed in the space above the crown of my head, and which penetrated into my interior, and that in that hole, was, well . . . God. And where I ended, and where God began, was a matter of degree.

If I dared approach that hole in my nature, that specific interior perforation in that veil which separated me from God, time would decelerate and my sense of self would re-distribute, and my consciousness would spike as I entered a zone of hyper-reality, a world where complete stillness and perfect motion were resolved in God.

My willingness to face God was always the trigger.

As I gave myself over to God's attention, the magnitude of my consciousness increased. And the more aware I was of God, the more aware I was.

Dramatically more aware. One can be, seemingly, infinitely more aware as the God of Infinity is grasped.

Grasped by the unmanifest in us that connects us to the Unmanifest that underpins and exceeds the world.

This is why religious practitioners of all traditions contemplate God in his manifest forms, as a stepping stone to His unmanifest Nature. Why the Muslim mystics, the Sufis, recite the attributes of God. Why yogis contemplate the Infinite. Why Buddhists contemplate the Void.

To confront their nature with the Infinite, and to require their own growth thereby.

We grow in response to the demands of the Infinite, in the desire to try to meet It halfway, to encompass nothing less than Infinity.

Whatever you conceive Infinity to be, go out to It!

✳ Time Is Modified by Consciousness

IN THE MONTHS AND YEARS that followed my initial experience of God, there were frequent experiences of reality becoming suddenly more Real, and with it a sudden increase in my level of consciousness. My sense of self would redistribute itself; would see the larger world as an extension of myself, felt the trees as much as part of me as my hands. And time . . .

Time slowed dramatically.

Would watch the slow motion of the wings of birds in flight.

Time is a function of consciousness. The more awake one is, the slower time progresses.

But we all know this already, right? I mean, compare your last eight seconds of orgasm to your last eight seconds of sleep.

Which went by quicker? During which were you more aware?

The eight seconds of orgasm went ten thousand times slower than the eight seconds of sleep. Maybe a million times slower. The only difference in these eight seconds was in your level of awareness. Increased consciousness slows down the passage of time.

One of the great attractions of sexual activity is the increase in awareness that it engenders.

Were the birds your orgasm, you would be able to watch their wings in motion. Were you that awake.

❀ Sexual Union Has Aspects of Spiritual Union

AS I HAVE ALREADY MENTIONED, my experience had certain similarities to what happens at orgasm.

And I'm afraid more than just certain similarities.

I would assert that both are features of one process. That sexual union is a lesser analogue to the larger union, which is man (or woman) and God.

Many religions consider sexual union to have a sacred aspect. Some practices, such as Tantrism, significantly focus on sexual union. Within Christianity, marriage is considered a sacrament, a physical union interwoven with the sacred.

Undoubtedly, the sacred nature of marriage within Christianity is based on more than sexual union. It's also the union of heart to heart, and mind to mind.

Sexual union also carries with it profound aspects of spiritual union.

* * *

If sexuality is in some sense an aspect of spirituality, then why are priests, monks, and holy men and women of all sorts celibate? Or at least are supposed to be?

It is worthwhile noting that when my union with God occurred, I was a very celibate seventeen-year-old. A case might be made that the events which led to union were, in some sense, a sublimation of the sexual impulse.

This spiritual potentiality created by the sublimation of the sexual impulse may account for the historical celibacy of many religious practitioners, from vestal virgins, to Buddhist monks, to Catholic priests.

Of course I should also note that judging by all the scandals that have gone on, and continue to go on, improper sublimation of the sexual impulse by monks and priests can lead to things much worse than loss of spiritual potentiality.

Like hell, I suppose, if hell there be.

❋ Sexual Union Is Knowledge-Producing

SEXUALITY TENDS TO BE interwoven with many aspects of religious and spiritual expression, and is an aspect of one process that leads to union with God, and to knowledge of the underpinnings of Reality.

My experience of God was knowledge-producing. Knowledge of God, of myself, and of the nature of things.

I have said that sexual union is an aspect of a larger spiritual process. Is sexual union, then, knowledge-producing in a spiritual sense?

Well, in the ages before the talk-show, when matters were put more delicately, knowledge was used to describe a sexual encounter: She knew him. He knew her. Was this description simply a euphemism for the sexual act, or was it somehow accurate? That knowledge proceeded from the act? A knowledge deeper than that of sexual sophistication?

My answer is yes, yes, yes. I note with interest a change in the spiritual outlook of the newly married and believe that they acquire a deeper knowledge of themselves, and the world, and God.

But this transformation, being a widely experienced and common one, is underrated, under-noted, and so bound up with the coarseness of our media today that this deep measure of God's providence to people's inner lives goes all but unnoticed.

❀ Saint Bonaventure, the Seraphic Doctor

I HAD STARTED LOOKING for a college a few weeks before my experience, and after it, my search turned toward finding a Catholic college that had a monastery affiliated with it.

I figured that if anyone knew about what was happening to me, it was likely to be someone dressed in a cassock, or similar funky garb.

And so I attended St. Bonaventure University, near Olean, New York. St. Bonas is set in the beginnings of the Appalachians which start in southwestern New York.

Thomas Merton had hung out there, as he was preparing to enter a Trappist monastery.

St. Bonaventure was run by Franciscans, and there was a friary on campus, with perhaps eighty friars. Up the road, atop a large hill, was the St. Elizabeth Motherhouse, which housed a hundred nuns. There was also a large seminary that housed several dozen candidates for the priesthood.

There were two Catholic churches within a mile of campus, neither of which had anything to do with the college; and then there were the altars in the friary, the motherhouse, and the seminary.

Across the Allegheny River, some of the younger friars had convinced the order to allow them to build a small hideaway in the woods, and four of them had moved out there and were playing hermit, if you can realistically be a hermit, four persons to a hideaway.

Semi-hermits.

The school also housed the Ockham Institute, the designated worldwide study center for the works of William of Ockham, famous medieval philosopher. A half-dozen friars from Belgium and France and elsewhere worked at the institute.

There was a church and three chapels on campus, for use by the less than two thousand students.

It was way Catholic.

Now, Saint Bonaventure himself was a Franciscan, and a profound mystic, the "Seraphic Doctor," whose repute has been largely overshadowed by the reputation of Saint Francis, the founder of the order.

I'm sure Saint Bonaventure doesn't mind. I mean, by definition, saints don't have that competitive thing going on.

One of Bonaventure's most important works is *The Soul's Journey into God*. Not exactly Eckhart, but awfully good. I especially like chapter seven:

ON
SPIRITUAL AND MYSTICAL ECSTASY
IN WHICH REST IS GIVEN TO OUR
INTELLECT
WHEN THROUGH ECSTASY OUR
AFFECTION
PASSES OVER ENTIRELY INTO GOD

It's surprising that Bonaventure is not read more. He's certainly not holding anything back.

Perhaps he should have been more coy.

✸ Remain a Catholic

I WAS RAISED, educated, and remain a Catholic.

I find that if I do not become overly litigious about scripture, I can make my experience accord well with the gospel. And thankfully, Catholics are not now biblical literalists.

I must confess, however, that my understanding of the gospels is my own, and is in some sense quite different from the consensual understanding of most Catholics. My viewpoint is even further in distance from that of the Christian fundamentalists. There is a balance in most forms of Christianity, a tension as to whether Christianity is the religion *of* Jesus or the religion *about* Jesus. I'm to the *of* side of the spectrum, and am probably somewhat away from the belief set of the average Catholic, and even further downwind from the fundamentalists.

Were these the Late Middle Ages, I undoubtedly would have been burned at the stake by the age of thirty-one. And perhaps as early as age seventeen.

Nonetheless, I remain a Catholic, but not prejudicially so. I mean, who could possibly be prejudicially Catholic these days with all the scandals going on? Please.

✳ God's Nature Is to Be Provident to All People

I HAVE HAD THE GOOD FORTUNE over the years to meet a number of people who manifest a great spiritual weight, and not one of them would have claimed that his or her own path was the only path to the Ultimate. All of them far too intensely sense the providence of God to ever make that error.

They might debate the effectiveness of one path versus another, but they would never doubt that a great many paths lead to that place of Light.

Speaking for myself, as I read the Vedas, or the aphorisms of Patanjali, or the Buddhist sutras, or the writings of the Zen Buddhists, or the writings of the Sufis, or the letters of Paul, I find myself quickly in over my head, paddling in deep water. But God, I love that water. Love it, love it. Know it to be all water.

There is no shortage of great spiritual wisdom. It's everywhere, modulated only by our ability to absorb it. This issue is always within us.

God is that provident. Not only is He everywhere, but so is His wisdom, and He speaks alike to all of humanity who will listen, in accordance with their cultural biases, backgrounds, and readiness to learn. It is God's nature to be provident to all people, and He is true to His nature. His Excellence demands such providence.

Could you expect less of Him?

Those people who imagine that they drink from God's well, and who are pleased to imagine that others do not, are poster children for the sin of pride.

One need not embrace all religions if one embraces tolerance. Keep to whatever tradition you keep. It's far better to follow your own tradition than to become a spiritual dilettante, browsing lightly near and far. Depth counts for more than breadth.

My advice is this: Within your own understanding, make for your own deep water and linger there. Dive down into the cool black, as the mood strikes you.

There is more to this ocean than any of our buckets can hold, and yet we spend our time vying over which bucket.

≺≺ 3 ≻≻

Mind-Poise

❦ The King of Yogas

WHEN I WAS AT ST. BONAVENTURE, I began to study yoga in earnest.

I also began to drink beer in earnest; Budweiser, the King of Beers. And began to smoke cigarettes in earnest, as well.

It was an earnest time.

The first book that I purchased after my experience was a fortuitous choice, the book *Practical Yoga* by Professor Ernest Wood, first published in 1948, and reprinted in the 1970s, and now sadly out of print. This was only a practical book if one considers enlightenment to be a practical undertaking.

And although the road to enlightenment may in fact be successfully undertaken, I hesitate, even now, to describe it as a practical undertaking.

Practical undertakings are things like knowing how to replace the water pump in your car when the old one starts to chirp, for example.

Professor Wood's book had no pictures, no diagrams, and needed none, as it had nothing to do with yoga as it is currently taught in the West. Rather, it was a very erudite commentary on the aphorisms of Patanjali, an abstruse collection of compressed wisdom.

As with Zen writings, the aphorisms are notably pithy.

For example, II, 9: "Possessiveness, which is firmly established even in the learned, carries on by its own relish."

But it was a very exciting book for me. Not that I understood it all, then or now. But the exciting thing that I discovered was that the book described, in a roundabout sense, some of the reasons that

I had had my experience of God. It outlined the process, spoke to me about some of the things I already knew, as all good books should.

The aphorisms of Patanjali form the basis of what is known as Raja Yoga, the king of the yogas.

It is a primarily mental yoga, and only briefly touches on subjects familiar to Hatha yogis, such as posture and breath. And although there is much advice about the sort of life one should lead to prepare oneself to do Raja Yoga, the heart of the practice is in the triple action of: Concentration. Meditation. Contemplation.

The triple action of these three elements is called *mind-poise*.

✳ Mind-Poise

MIND-POISE IS THE ACTIVE use of the mind to receive revelation. One begins mind-poise by developing the skill to bind the mind to a certain subject, to think about the subject fully in a very ordered manner, and, upon conclusion of this thorough investigation, to hold all facts aloft, in some sense, at one moment, in the act of contemplation.

And in contemplation, there is revelation.

So this mind-poise is important stuff.

Our good Professor Wood uses the rose as an example of how to practice mind-poise.

Having comfortably seated yourself and established regular breathing, give complete thought to, for example, a rose.

Think all thoughts that can be thought about a rose. Try to imagine every rose you have ever seen, every rose you have ever smelled.

Think about where roses grow best. What we know about their soil requirements, their need for water and light, how to protect them in winter. Their historical origins, the literary references to them . . . the Rose Parade.

Don't let me kid you. This is a laborious process. This is what Patanjali refers to as meditation. Active thought. Not just sitting there passively, with some level of suspension of thought, although this practice also has its significant uses.

Once you have trained your mind to actively focus on something, you also tend toward excellence in the ability to empty your mind. Both fullness and emptiness have their uses.

The final step in this process is the contemplation of the rose. It is contemplation that pays off.

But I shall let Professor Wood speak:

With this knowledge, it becomes clear that in Meditation and Contemplation we have the fulfillment of faculty, not its dissolution, and the reception of revelation. Contemplation is a kind of worship, reached through a Meditation in which we value experience, and Concentration which grips the things of sense with the hand of a brother.

Earlier I wrote:

Anyway, as a teenager, I wrote poems, and I would go out into the countryside and "be poetical."

What this meant, in practice, was that I would go to some remote spot, and would clear my mind and be fully there, and would sense something. That something was always an explicit something. A specific taste. Not a vaporous thing at all.

Now, what I had apparently learned to do was to achieve a certain level of mind-poise, "the reception of revelation" of which Professor Wood speaks.

Coming over the top of that green hill on that April day, my mind was concentrated by the vision opening before me: rolling sky, swaying branches, red buds, earth smell, rain on my face, winding road, stone walls. I opened myself to the world, to the unity suggested. Contemplated without caution. Achieved mind-poise on that unity.

Professor Wood knew what I am talking about. He writes of mind-poise:

Now a moment will come when new light will be revealed—call it intuition, some effect whereby one becomes aware of what one could not catch before. Intuition dawns, or sometimes flashes, and with it the ecstasy that means more than life.

MIND-POISE

✳ Mind-Poise and the Organ of Spiritual Perception

WHAT IS THE RELATIONSHIP between mind-poise as described by Patanjali and the operation of the organ of spiritual perception that I discussed earlier, which forms the basis of the poetic experience?

Both the revelation of mind-poise and the revelation that informs the poetic experience occur as part of one faculty, which proceeds from the heart. But though the faculty used is the same in both cases, the intention that underlies mind-poise is somewhat different from the intention that underlies the poetic realization.

It's kind of like the difference between building strong muscles by, say, working daily on a farm; and by building muscles by lifting weights. In both cases, the same muscles are used, but in working around a farm, the development of muscles is a by-product of the work, whereas in weight lifting, the intention of the work is to develop muscles.

In mind-poise, one works toward revelation based on one's intention, one's desire for a specific revelation—say, to understand "roseness." In poetic realization, one perceives whatever revelation is inherent in the experience in which one is engaged. It's the difference between walking in one's garden, where one has been diligently planting, watering, and weeding . . . and taking a walk in the countryside and finding whatever is.

✳

❋ Distilled into One Feeling

LET ME DIGRESS for a moment, before I discuss how all this works together, and how revelation comes from this process.

I am old enough, now, that I can sense large portions of my youth as a single feeling.

Oh, if so inclined, I can go back to the specifics, year by year: how my home smelled when breakfast was cooking, my best friend in fifth grade, that time we went on vacation, alone after the fire.

But somehow, I can also capture it all as a single feeling. My life as a flavor. That thing that was my youth.

As Mr. Eliot says in his *Four Quartets*:

> *Home is where one starts from. As we grow older*
> *The world becomes stranger, the pattern more complicated*
> *Of dead and living. Not the intense moment*
> *Isolated, with no before and after,*
> *But a lifetime burning in every moment*
> *And not the lifetime of one man only*
> *But of old stones that cannot be deciphered.*

You know how you get a certain feeling from a certain song? Uplifted, or brooding, or a sweet movement between the two? Angry? Wistful? A feeling for which there is no specific word? Well, when I think of my youth, I get a feeling like that, but more convolved. Richer.

* * *

So back to the rose. To do mind-poise on the rose, you must sit and imagine a specific rose, or view an actual rose, and then bring all the thinking that you have done about the rose to bear upon your contemplation.

To be able to bring "all that you have thought about" into contemplation, you must reduce all those thoughts into one feeling. To feel about a rose in the same way that you feel about that song, in a manner that is intensely focused on the rose.

And as you successfully do this, something profound will awaken in you, in regard to roseness.

You'll not have the same relationship to roses, ever again. Roses will have taken on a deeper reality, and the next rose you encounter—say, in a gray October garden—will give you a shudder of delight, in some deep inwardness.

But I should let Mr. Eliot speak:

> *We shall not cease from exploration*
> *And the end of all our exploring*
> *Will be to arrive where we started*
> *And know the place for the first time.*
> *Through the unknown, remembered gate*
> *When the last of earth left to discover*
> *Is that which was the beginning;*
> *At the source of the longest river*
> *The voice of the hidden waterfall*
> *And the children in the apple-tree*
> *Not known, because not looked for*
> *But heard, half-heard, in the stillness*
> *Between two waves of the sea.*
> *Quick now, here, now, always—*
> *A condition of complete simplicity*
> *(Costing not less than everything)*
> *And all shall be well and*

All manner of things shall be well
When the tongues of flame are in-folded
Into the crowned knot of fire
And the fire and the rose are one.

* * *

Whew.

✳ Poetic Sensibility

THE SENSIBILITY UNDERLYING the poem is based on a sensibility underlying the world.

The poetic moments of which I have often spoken are moments of specific revelation, and the revelation counts for much more than the poem, by a long shot.

This revelation occurs as a result of the workings of the Spirit; whereas the poem is but an artifact, a footprint of the Spirit's forward progress.

The revelation counts for more than the poem. And such revelation depends on the cultivation of a refined heart.

There are many bad poets in the world who nonetheless have a refined heart, who have a knowing that they cannot seem to translate into words.

It is teachers and friends and colleagues and editors who judge the merits of poems. But it is God who rejoices in the knowing heart!

* * *

Consider Rumi. Consider the Persian poets, who are also considered to be great sages. Hafiz. Attar. Why are they all considered to be great mystics? I think it is because there is very little difference between the sensibility that leads to poetry and the sensibility that is enjoyed by the mystic. Very little difference, other than intensity, between that sensibility and the sensibility of the fisherman, hip-deep in a stream at dawn.

It all depends on a certain inner poise. On the openness of that organ of spiritual perception.

What else can mind-poise do? Patanjali gives dozens of examples:

By mind-poise on the triple transformation comes knowledge of past and future.

By mind-poise upon the mental images arises knowledge of other minds.

From bringing into consciousness the habit-molds gives knowledge of previous life conditions.

On the pit of the throat, the cessation of hunger and thirst.

On the light in the head, the seeing of the adepts.

From mind-poise upon the connection between the ear and the ether arises higher hearing.

Control of the forms of matter arises from mind-poise on their solid state, character, finer forms, connections, and utility or functions.

The triple action of concentration, meditation and contemplation on these subjects is called mind-poise with seed, because mind-poise is sought in order to yield tangible results.

Mind-poise upon God or the Infinite is called seedless.

Either way, mind-poise is an active process. A long process. A process of years, not a weekend. An avocation, and not something to embark on lightly.

It brings to bear a process that is in some ways very dissimilar to the process of meditation in the West.

But it also is found everywhere in the West by another name.

✳ An Orientation for Life

UNDERSTANDING THE PROCESS of mind-poise, and its potentiality for producing spiritual growth, provides one with an avenue that leads to a fuller spiritual life.

I am not suggesting that one start up a practice of Raja Yoga, sitting down for extended periods and formally concentrating, meditating and contemplating various subjects. That's certainly not my intent. Raja Yoga is a very demanding yoga which requires the best of you; and to be a fine yogi requires the same sort of dedication in time and intensity as does a bicycle racer or marathon runner. Raja Yoga requires one to spend daily time working on one's ability to direct the mind where one wills, and it is hard work in the same way that running ten miles is hard work. Maybe harder.

The few people who start up on Raja Yoga tend to stick with it for a while, and then to slough off, and then quickly to do it not at all. Similar to many diet and exercise fads.

The good news is that the practice of mind-poise does not require the practice of Raja Yoga. There is still plenty of room for mind-poise within the overall strategy that you use to prosecute your life. Still plenty of room for it in your basic orientation. In your walking-around mind. In your scratching-your-ass mind.

* * *

As an example of its more expansive use . . . I was asked some years ago, by a Sufi of my acquaintance, what philosophy I used in raising my two boys, who are now grown to fine men.

✳

✳ Its Use in Raising Children

I WROTE THE following in reply:

Since my experience, I've always felt that Reality, from a human standpoint, was a faceted thing, and that each facet required a different ontological approach, each with a particular strength and weakness, and that no one approach should be allowed exclusivity. This seems to have been a major human problem at all times. As Blake said, "The crow wished that everything was black, the owl, that everything was white."

So in regards to my kids, when I would talk about a particular tree, I would try, over time, to talk about its biology, about the physics latent within the distribution of weight in its canopy, about the math within the physics, its orientation to the garden, its effects on the things which grow in its shade . . . I painted a picture of it . . . and then we'd tap it for syrup in the springtime, for our pancakes. (I did not tell them that, given the right conditions, it would greet them in the morning, as one took one's morning walk through the garden.) So my goal with the kids was to have a certain something within them not calcify. And to be awake in a fully human sense, and to not wander about in a re-circulating dream as so many seem to do. But my lessons with them have always focused on how to tell, say, good loam, and about the Buddha not at all.

❋ Mind-Poise Is Behind All Success

EVERYWHERE YOU LOOK, you find people who are passionate about their normal pursuits in the world. The scientist who loves her research. The carpenter who really knows the feel of the wood he is working, who has a certain knowledge of its possibilities. The nurse who understands that particular something under life, in the outcomes of her patients.

Average pursuits, perhaps; but there are no average passions.

Such people have concentrated on a given portion of reality, have meditated long and deeply over it, and have discovered, in their passion and intuition . . . It.

Have discovered a sense of God, although they often do not call it God.

Ever wonder why the Japanese, for example, might refer to a traditional potter as a spiritual master, and his pots as spiritual masterpieces?

They understand that to know *It* is also to know IT.

Anyone who is half-good at anything, or half-passionate about anything, is already half-doing *It*.

❦ My Grandfather's Beatitudes

IT MUST BE TIME for a poem:

> "Blest be the gardener: for
>   his eyes may rest upon
>   the late afternoon horizon."

> "Blest is him who breathes:
>   for he may breathe early
>   fog swept from receding pine."

> "Blessed are they that pulled
>   weeds amongst the thorns, and in
>   baking, relentless weather:
>   their efforts did yield
>   this remarkable
>   day.

> From that far rusting gate
>   to the new,

> for it is ours."

❈ Like a Jacket on a Hook

BASED ON Professor Wood's book, I began to practice Raja Yoga as a freshman in college, still seventeen. Drinking age was eighteen.

I ultimately ran into another student who was a fine Hatha yogi. As he taught me Hatha Yoga, I taught him Raja Yoga. He was a better Hatha yogi than I was a Raja yogi, and I think I got the better of the bargain.

This other yogi and I would get up at 6:00 AM and do an hour or two of yoga together. He taught me Hatha Yoga postures and breathing, while I tried to show him something about concentration and contemplation.

Getting up at 6:00 AM was never my thing, however, and this lasted for only a couple of months. (My personal biorhythms are those of a tavern owner. Personal sacrifice is personal sacrifice and all, but my God, 6:00 AM is 6:00 AM. There's never been a good 6:00 AM in my life.)

In the few months we worked together, I picked up a smattering of postures and exercises that I liked and started doing them regularly, but in the late evening. And, of course, I continued with my contemplation.

I tried to teach the other yogi an exercise whereby one learns to hang one's attention on one thing, like one hangs a jacket on a hook, and to keep it there without undue will, hung, as it were, by itself.

All kinds of interesting things happen once one has learned to do this.

I long ago lost touch with this fellow, and I don't know if what I tried to teach him ever took root.

I do know that what he taught me has stayed with me these thirty-odd years.

Based on the yoga he taught, I have practiced many basic postures regularly over the years, but none of the really hard ones. He also taught me something about the chakras, although the chakras seemed pretty abstract to him at the time.

✸ The Chakras

THE CHAKRAS, a term that I understand is translatable from the Sanskrit as "wheels," form part of the underlying philosophical structure on which Hatha Yoga is based. Each one of the postures within Hatha is targeted toward having an effect on one or more of the chakras.

The chakras are kind of like vortices that span different dimensionalities. Centers of psycho-spiritual energies. When one thinks of someone as "having heart" or "having a fire in the belly" or just being good and horny, that person is, according to the yogis, experiencing a predominance of one of the chakras' dimensionalities.

Many New Age works refer to the chakras, and there is much discussion of them in deeper yoga books and in some books about the more esoteric aspects of Hinduism. A very long Hindu religious tradition also has been finely interwoven with the chakras.

Let me quote Ajit Mookerjee, as he discusses one of the chakras:

Visuddha, meaning "pure," is located at the juncture of the spinal column and the medula oblongata behind the throat (laryngeal plexus). Its sixteen smoky-purple petals bear the sixteen vowels a, ā, i, ī, u, ū, ṛ, ṝ, ḷ, ḹ, e, ai, o, au, am, ah. Within its pericarp is a white circle, and a triangle inscribed with the seed mantra Haṃ. The presiding deity is Sadāśiva as Ardhvanārīśvara (his androgynous aspect); the right half of his body is white representing Śiva, and the left half is golden representing Śakti. The deity is five-faced, three-eyed, holding a trident, an axe, a sword, a vajra (thunderbolt), fire, Ananta Serpent, a bell, a goad, and a noose, and is making the gestures of dispelling fear.

Over its long cultural/historical association, a large amount of anecdotal information has become attached to the chakras, like barnacles, and it's sometimes hard to pry the religious beliefs and the reality of their experience apart.

I must confess, it is hard for me, as a non-Hindu, to imagine how even a god could dispel fear while making an appearance with five faces, three eyes, and many hands . . . which hold a trident, an ax, a serpent, and a noose.

But to be fair, I have also never attempted mind-poise on it.

✳ Kundalini

PROFESSOR WOOD, back when his book was first published, in 1948, wrote about the chakras, and about kundalini, the force that activates them; arising, as it does, through their "petals":

There is a school of yoga, closely associated with Hatha Yoga, which prescribes meditations in what are called the centers (chakras). Six of these centers are mentioned . . . . The culmination of the whole process arrives when the coiled force is taken beyond all the six centers into the "thousand-petaled lotus" in the top part of the head, where it confers on man the highest intuitions and realizations. The name Laya Yoga (laya means latent) is given to this method, as it uses the coiled force latent in the body.

Earlier I wrote of my experience:

As the joy in me grew at a geometric rate, I recognized that something was happening—that the joy was an energy from outside me, flowing into me from a great distance, and then was translated upward.

It was like a series of notes being struck as the energy rushed upward. And my being changed in a series of fixed steps. I was accelerated.

The series of notes being struck was the result of a certain energy proceeding through the chakras. There was a fixed progression in the energy, a mathematical relationship, between one state and the next. Mr. Mookerjee informs me that the number of petals on each of the chakras, as they ascend, changes from 4 to 6; 6 to 10; 10 to 12; 12 to 16; then 16 to 2; and 2 to 1000.

I have no idea if the numeric relationships given for these chakras have a direct relationship with what I experienced, but I do find it interesting that there are numbers associated with the chakras, and that their values rise rapidly.

In a moment, the energy rose to my throat, and I suddenly became outside my body, looking at the exterior surfaces of my body from all around, from each angle, from many distances, at the same instant. I looked deeply into my own eyes.

That, I suppose, could have been the start of that thousand-petaled part.

✸ The Person as a Cluster of Chakras

MANY THINGS HAVE BEEN WRITTEN about the chakras that make them seem very esoteric, or wrapped in great mystery, or just plain bizarre.

But just about everyone has a daily familiarity with at least several of the chakras, and experiences them directly, and experiences them in ways that are so common and so natural that they are barely observed at all.

Three of the chakras are the place at the spine where sensations from the genitals gather; the heart; and the head.

But let me quote John Hiatt in "Little Head":

I'm dirty as a manhole cover
I'm looking for my long lost lover
She turned me out an' now I'm sinkin'
I'm just so easily led when the little head does the thinkin'

And think it does, within a certain range of possibilities.

Daily we hear stories about a famous or powerful person who has blundered into some scandal as a result of his or her being so easily led. Such people, we often think, should have known better.

And often they do know better. At least their big head does.

And then there is the influence of the heart. The less-subtle heart; that oxygenated, emotional heart.

Knowing beauty, whether rough or fine, flickers of love, the mystic chords of memory where the other's smile is like the smile past, on that beach long ago or that morning before the fire, that longing . . .

Pack in close proximity the genitals, heart, and head, and no wonder there is so much scandal in the world. Really, how could there not be?

The point I wish to make is that each one of these orientations, each of these viewpoints upon the world, is associated with one of the chakras, and each of these viewpoints is different.

Each of these viewpoints reflects a fundamentally different consciousness.

The rational mind thinks; the heart feels; the sexual snarls like Shakespeare's "beast with two backs." Each responds to different aspects of reality in ways not well understood, nor well respected, by the others.

Each has its own language. Each has an ongoing dialogue within that particular language, but each also holds a dialogue of sorts with the others. Each has an orientation that connects with Reality, that is analogous to what is going on in the others.

In understanding the chakras, the most fundamental understanding is that they represent how we really experience the world.

We experience the world in a number of different modes, with a set of awarenesses that are distributed through us and that we synthesize into an overall understanding of ourselves.

We are a cluster of seemingly separate perspectives, speaking separate languages, although we seldom think of ourselves like that. Instead, we tend to think of ourselves as a rational mind, which we consider to be our real selves, our true nature.

❧ Pre-Katrina Norleans Yoga

HATHA YOGA IS A PHYSICAL SCIENCE for the differential stimulation of chakras, or groups of chakras. Different schools of Hatha Yoga emphasize different approaches to their stimulation; or have a focus on specific clusters of the chakras; or differ in how their larger energies are developed and deployed.

Sometimes the yoga becomes as specific as is the person, as it is practiced over long periods of time.

Thirty years after I first learned yoga, I still do Hatha Yoga daily, or mostly daily. Although I must confess that it has become a shiftless kind of yoga; a Pre-Katrina, New Orleans kind of yoga.

There are many schools of yoga. Kundalini. Kripalu. Kriya. And that's just the Ks.

Were I to teach my brand of yoga, I would call it the New Orleans school of Yoga. Norleans yoga.

Under the Ns.

✸ Perfection of Worship

MY YOGA IS COMPATIBLE with beer and cigars. It requires no particular clothing or props, and so may be practiced by the street person.

Not many types of yoga, outside of India, can claim that.

My yoga uses very simple postures, and does not involve getting even those simple postures to look particularly like the pictures in those many books about Hatha Yoga.

In Norleans Yoga, if you can look good while doing it, good enough to rate a picture . . . then you're clearly not doing it right. Norleans Yoga looks like a Brooklyn matron performing heavy cleaning, at a church.

In Norleans Yoga, the point of the postures is to accompany a kind of worship. A kind of worship that is modulated, somehow, by the posture.

What counts in Norleans Yoga is not perfection of form, but perfection of worship.

In regard to the various postures, it succeeds when one gets a certain effect out of a given posture, with a certain use of breath, when accompanied by an intent of worship.

It does not rely on what the posture looks like. The point is the effect, not the perfection of posture. Posture be damned.

Most Hatha Yoga in the West has moved away from being a spiritual discipline and into something that looks very much like bodybuilding.

A type of athleticism that may be judged, as other forms of athleticism are judged, like gymnastics, or skating, or diving. This requires working on one's yoga in a competitive sense, so that one's routine might score a 9.5, 9.6, 9.8, 9.5, 9.5, 9.6 from some astral set of judges. Based on degree of difficulty, fluidity of transition, perfect immobility of posture at difficult junctures, the creative interjection(!) of mantras . . . showing the flexibility and litheness of the young and lean yoga body, outfitted with stylish yoga fashion-wear. Displaying a competitor who is both spiritual *and hip*.

In Norleans yoga, we don't put up with any of that crap.

Oh, please don't get me wrong.

It's that New Orleans is just the wrong town for a yoga body.

And also, that the only spandex you find there is on the hookers, who admittedly wear it very well.

ᴕ

❊ The Energy Is Instructive

IN NORLEANS YOGA, first and foremost, one must be attentive to God. Every other aspect depends on this.

Norleans yoga is generally done by oneself. Doing yoga with others unavoidably creates a social occasion, and this social occasion competes with the prayerful and contemplative orientation toward God that is necessary for this yoga.

The premise of this yoga is simple.

The chakras are viewed as a series of levers or tumblers, which must be thrown, or opened in the presence of God, and when one does this, a flow of a certain energy begins to ripple through one, and this energy is instructive.

That's it.

As George Harrison writes:

> I'm a Pisces fish and the river runs
> through my soul
>
> And I'll be swimming until I can find
> those waters
>
> That one unbounded ocean of bliss
> That's flowing through your parents,
> sons and daughters
>
> But still an easy thing for us to miss

Is easy to miss when one does yoga as a social situation, as a student or a teacher.

Is easy to miss when one focuses on the outward form rather than the inward effect. And when one is not attentive to God.

It is the attention to God, you see, that provides the pull, that starts the flow. A river only runs, you see, because it has direction.

God provides the direction. Without attention to God, one can be only a swamp, not a river.

To become a Norleans yogi, one practices a variety of postures and breathing techniques in God's presence, and after each posture, one spends a good deal of time focusing within the body, within the pattern of energy distributed through the body and beyond, so as to discern what effect the exercise had.

The skill that is developed is the recognition of the pattern of energy that extends throughout, and beyond the body. There is a distribution of energy in the body which makes the heart to beat and the lungs to breathe, and which allows us to dance. If one tries, one may sense how that energy moves through the body. The point of doing a yoga posture is to change the pattern, to change the status quo in positive ways, to make it easier to sense the energy pattern by changing it, adding novelty to it. It's hard to be perceptive about the status quo.

✱ You Cannot Make It Flow

THE POINT OF NORLEANS YOGA is to learn to recognize that pattern of energy in the body and to learn how to change it. When one is aware of the pattern of one's own energy and can monitor that energy in real time, one may start modifying the traditional postures to get the maximum effect from them. This results, over time, in a set of personal postures that may bear only a slight resemblance to classical asanas. These postures are unique to the person doing them and change, day by day, as the need dictates. Until one is so attuned to one's energy that it may be adjusted just by a change in the posture of the hands.

And when the energy within the body is aligned in a certain way and one is attentive to God, a flow may begin which is instructive. A river may run through one's soul. And where does a river start? Where does it end?

You may find something within you that starts in a place outside yourself and ends in a place outside yourself. A river within you that connects you to both.

And it is not, by the way, even your river.

You can impede its flow, but you cannot make it flow.

You must depend on God for that.

✳ Inflamed Chakras

AFTER MY EXPERIENCE of God, I had inflamed chakras.

Were I able to consult with Saint Bonaventure, the Seraphic Doctor, he might have prescribed some sort of spiritual salve, I suppose.

As a result of this spiritual inflammation, my consciousness was volatile, and I was subject to a variety of spiritual or esoteric phenomena for many years after; and still somewhat am, I'm afraid.

The most repetitive of these phenomena was an odd temporal/ consciousness distortion: I felt as if there were a hole in my soul, on the other side of which was God. And as I attended to that hole, made mental approach to that hole, my consciousness quickened, and time slowed. The world would become increasingly more particular, more silent, more real; and then It would suddenly intensify, and time would slow to a fraction of its normal meter as the world moved toward revelation. Subsisting in glory.

There were flashes of psychic phenomena as well, small visual bits of precognition about matters usually trivial; or the occasional telepathic burp of someone else's thought made manifest.

And then there were, most dear to me, those moments of grace.

In ballet, the sense of grace involves the light and fluid motion of all the dancers in an intricate and reciprocal fashion, something that beautifully unfolds; and my moments of grace were like this. A reciprocal ballet of need, generosity and fulfillment; whereby my exotic needs were completely fulfilled by, say, some stray conversation; or when through my blundering, inchoate actions, someone else's problems was resolved in a manner whose outcome exceeded my best intentions.

I was aware, in these moments, of participating in God's mercy, most dear to me.

✳ Out-of-Body Experience

ONE AFTERNOON in my freshman year at St. Bonaventure, I spent an entire English class gamely trying to stay awake, and nearly failing. It was that kind of lecture.

After class I walked the quarter mile back to my dorm room and lay down on my bed, on my back. I was glad my roommate was out and I had a moment of peace.

I lay there for only a minute, and then I felt what can only be described as some strange, internal tug at the back of my neck. And then I went black. It was not like falling asleep, but rather as if that tug had immediately taken my consciousness.

Out of that unconsciousness, I was suddenly aware that I was aware, and was aware that I was not in my body, which was lying inert on the bed.

I was looking down at my body from above, which I guess is a kind of classically out-of-body thing to do. My perspective on the room was very odd.

It seemed to me that I had been out a while and had just returned from somewhere.

And then I thought something to the effect of:

Well, time to get back into ol' stupid.

And as I thought this, I moved toward my body, turned, and went black. And awoke with a start on the bed.

✸

✹ Out of Body Experience Different from Mystical Experience

AS YOU MIGHT RECALL, I had also been out-of-body during my experience of God, when I was like a sentient cloud. This second out-of-body experience was very different.

In my first experience, I no longer had what might be called a human mind, and I had no single perspective, but rather a multiplicity of potential perspectives.

In this second experience, I had a relationship to mind similar to the mind that I experience as I write this book. Like a human, I was experiencing from one perspective, was perceiving with a sense like seeing and not with the unified perception that was part of my experience of God. I had no particularly elevated sense of God.

I have always considered this second experience to be somewhat trivial in comparison to the moment of my effacement in God.

✺ Brain Does Not Contain Mind

OVER THE PAST THIRTY YEARS, I have been freed of my body on a handful of occasions.

On a couple of those occasions, I had classic out-of-body experiences. On the others, I was freed of my physicality during contemplation.

Occasionally during deep contemplation, I have found myself to be thinking extraordinarily well. To be thinking far beyond the range of my normal thought. Not even aware that the linkages between mind and body have been broken.

What immense grandeur there is in the Greater Mind!

In these instances, I became aware of reentering my body only as I observed my capacity to think: slow to a creep, constrict, and fragment into a slog of one thought at a time.

Like I now write this book, mostly.

There are still many practical and scientifically minded people in the world who believe that, in some inexplicable way, the brain creates thought. Thought as explained by neural connections. Thought as mapped by PET scans. Thought as electrical fields within the brain. Thought as quantum effects of the atoms within the brain. And when the brain goes, thought goes, too.

Goodbye, goodbye.

While the brain certainly lights up in a thinking person, I do not, of course, believe that thought originates within it. Or more accurately, I believe that there is a waltz, of sorts, going on between the brain and the intellection of the thinking soul. And between the thinking soul, and the Greater Mind.

The brain acts as a conduit between dimensions. Which is in itself a remarkable thing.

The world of ideas, the world of the mind, is the context within which physical reality manifests itself.

The physical world depends on the mind, and not vice versa.

What scientists like to think of as physical law is not just some inexplicable set of relationships between phenomena, but is mind. Call it what you will. Consistent willed behavior, but behavior nonetheless.

But where was I?

Oh, yes, complaining about how I experienced the reintegration of my mind with my body, by witnessing the degradation of my mind during the process of reintegration.

When I say that I have occasionally discovered myself to be thinking extraordinarily well, I do not mean thinking marginally extraordinarily well. I mean a hundredfold. A thousandfold.

When thinking well, instead of thinking one thought at a time, one thinks a large bundle of thoughts at one time. Thoughts that are beautifully ordered, in a geometric or spiral relationship to one another. Thinking symphonically, as it were.

Taking a big bite of It.

And every thought in the bundle has a relationship to every other thought in the bundle, which creates a secondary set of thoughts that is a geometric expansion of the primary set.

I know all this is probably confusing.

✳ Unified Field Theory

LET ME USE Albert Einstein as an example.

Not that I understand physics even a little bit, mind you, so do not be intimidated.

But Einstein tried, as best I understand it, to create something called the unified field theory, which would explain the relationship of all physical phenomena as one equation. $E=MC^2$ for the entire universe, instead of just a piece of it.

Einstein was known to think about profound physics issues in terms of human experience. Would imagine himself standing in an elevator and wonder if he could tell whether he was in motion in the absence of gravity or just standing in a typical elevator on earth. Would imagine himself being on a train going at the speed of light. And other such imaginings.

Einstein was a physicist and knew about the properties of light under various circumstances; about the properties of energy, motion, and mass. He understood the ramifications of many key physical experiments that were going on during his life, was aware of the structure of the hypotheses that underpinned these experiments, and of the space of theoretic possibility that could allow each experimental result to modulate the coherent vision of reality that was emerging.

Einstein was also a mathematician and knew that whatever physical theory would be found to hold water would also hold water mathematically. He knew that the structure of mathematical relationships proved true would somehow mirror the relationships between matter, time, space, and energy.

Repetitive and corresponding truths.

And Einstein also had his theological or philosophical predilections.

He would not allow that God could be playing dice with the universe, for example.

Einstein never completed his work on the unified field theory. Couldn't pull it off.

Or, could not bring it back and get it down on paper.

Had Einstein been able to think about everything he knew about human experience, and physics, and mathematics, and philosophy all at the same time, he may have been able to actually see wherein the unified field theory lay.

Increased insight as a result of being able to hold aloft, at the same time, all the dimensions of a given problem.

I am no Einstein, but freed of my body, I could freely maintain an ongoing bundle of all my thoughts and find their existential ground, which in my now reduced state, I can dimly poke at, but not explain.

In these experiences, as my mind reengaged the mechanics of my brain, I found that my thoughts slowed down, as if I were wading through molasses; then break, and they become associated with words, which add their own distortions and biases. The tap turned to a drip.

Would become aware of the sheer chattering and noise of the mechanicality of the brain, as if one had somehow awakened in some textile mill that was running full bore.

✳ Back to Being Ol' Stupid

ABOUT THE ONLY common experience I have had during all of these out-of-body, or disengaged-from-body experiences, is the relative repugnance I have felt when rejoining the body:

Well, time to get back into ol' stupid.

I seem to share this feeling with Rumi.

Rumi talks about the friendship of a mouse and a frog in "The Long String," as translated by Coleman Barks:

> *Have mercy, said the mouse.*
> *I can't follow you into the water.*
> *Isn't there some way to keep in touch?*
> *A messenger? Some reminder?*

> *The two friends decided that the answer*
> *was a long, longing string, with one end tied*
> *to the mouse's foot and the other to the frog's,*
> *so that by pulling on it their secret connection*
> *might be remembered and the two could meet,*
> *as the soul does with the body.*

> *The froglike soul often escapes from the body*
> *and soars in the happy waters. Then the mouse body*
> *pulls on the string, and the soul thinks,*

> Damn.
> *I have to go back on the riverbank and talk*
> *with that scatterbrained mouse!*

The body is a friend to the soul, and provides us an opportunity for growth, and needs to be respected and protected on that dimension.

But when the mouse is gone, well . . .

We will be free to soar in the happy waters, with the other frogs.

✸ I'm Afraid Something Is Lost

WHEN WE DIE, there is something lost in the transition. Something is lost. Something for which we receive compensation.

The caterpillar and the butterfly are the classic examples of what I mean.

Just ask the butterpillar, after it comes out of its chrysalis, wings folded and wet, what it thinks of the state of affairs:

"But where are my many green feet, that I need to make my way from leaf to leaf? And where is my mouth to grind their sweet edges?"

Gone, my friend, they're gone. But God will provide you with compensations.

I have certain fundamentalist friends who think that they will be restored to their current bodies, at a robust age of their choosing, without warts and chipped teeth and such, when they are resurrected at the rapture, or at the end of time.

They also seem to envision heaven, I must confess, much like the Mall of America, but way bigger, and where everything is free. Where even the trash receptacles are covered with precious stones.

Ahem.

Far be it from me to attempt to stand between a person and the prosecution of his or her own religious destiny.

Therefore, let me interpose Saint Paul:

Someone may ask, "How are dead people raised, and what sort of body do they have when they come back?" They are stupid questions. Whatever you sow in the ground has to die before it is given new life and the thing that you sow is not what is going to come; you sow a bare grain, say of wheat or something like that, and then God gives it the sort of body that he has chosen; each sort of seed gets its own sort of body.

So. Look at a wheat seed.

Look at a wheat seedling.

Seed. Seedling.

Not much alike, are they?

Do you really think you will have fingers and toes, nose and belly button in the world to come?

✸ Spandalf

I am sometimes asked by my Christian fundamentalist friends for my opinion of what it is we do in the world-to-come; and I tell them, that I think that we spend a lot of time doing something that the angels call "Spandalf."

Spandalf is, spiritually speaking, the perfect intersection of croquet, ballet and hedge-trimming.

But it is, of course, done without the mallet, tu-tu or shears.

This world's the ball.

I'm Here to Stay

SINCE MY EFFACEMENT in God, I have never seriously considered that death may end my existence. I'm here to stay, for good or bad, but what I am may change, may change.

Oh, Lord, change me as I should be changed!

In Your own sweet time.

❦ A Shock

WHEN I FIRST STARTED to do Hatha Yoga, thirty years ago, I knew nothing about chakras.

I didn't have a particularly good sense of my internal energies, other than that I was afflicted with odd sensations that seemed to gather at certain places in my body, which were terribly strong after my experience.

There are some people who are completely comfortable in their skin. People who move with an animal-like grace. People who can tune their bodies like an instrument.

I was never one of those people.

Physically, I've always been pretty dim-witted.

When I first started to do Hatha Yoga, however, I noticed an effect right off. My consciousness shifted a little when I did certain postures. And I got to like the shifted result.

Also, doing Hatha seemed to help my back, which has always bothered me. I especially liked doing shoulder-stands, which seemed both to have an effect on my consciousness and to remedy my back pain. In the zeal of youth, I used to spend an unhealthy amount of time doing shoulder-stands, which are like headstands, but with your head on the ground and about ninety degrees to one side.

In my sophomore year of college, I would go the Campus Ministry Center, which had a number of small meditation rooms, and do Hatha and Raja Yoga for an hour or so almost every day.

One day, I was in one of those small rooms, alone, doing a shoulder-stand, when I had kind of a shock.

I felt a sudden flash of energy in my head. It was not a metaphysical thing but a physical thing, a sudden flash of white accompanied by a deep searing pain.

It was like getting hit in the head by a baseball. As metaphysical as that.

I got down from my shoulder-stand feeling woozy. Not myself. As if my neck had been stretched somehow.

I felt very spaced-out for the remainder of that day, and still strange the next, but after that I felt normal again. This happened a few days before I was to go home for Thanksgiving break.

It was several days before I decided to do yoga again, at home on Thanksgiving morning, the smell of cooking turkey in the air.

I did my usual yoga routine, Hatha first and then intending to contemplate next.

But when I did a shoulder-stand for too long, I again had that whacking flash, in my head, and again got down from my position feeling woozy.

I looked at my hands.

Which were suddenly strange.

I felt very off, tired and weird.

I told my parents that I wasn't feeling well, and then went back to bed. It is strange that I fell into a profound sleep, considering that I had been up only a couple of hours before starting my yoga.

Several hours later, I heard the sound of voices, and knew that a number of my relatives had come over for Thanksgiving dinner.

I dragged myself out of bed, ran my fingers through my hair, and went out to say hello.

As I entered my parents' living room fresh from sleep, I saw large nimbuses, or halos, or auras, or whatever surrounding everyone, including myself . . . my hands.

Energy gently sizzled off each person, interspersed with something like a fog, which was colored a subtle hue. Lines of force arced from every head.

I closed my eyes, shook my head, opened my eyes to find all this still there. I made some comment about not being fully awake.

My parents' living room kind of looked like the manger scene. Without baby Jesus; but now with Mary, Joseph, the wise men . . . wise women.

✻ Auras

WHEN I WENT TO BED that night, I kind of figured that the halo thing would disappear after a good night's sleep or a day or two of rest. I've had, I must confess, more bizarre things than that come and go.

But the next day, and the next day, and the next . . .

A week later, months later, a year later, I still saw auras and other odd things, although the halos became somewhat less vivid over time.

I see them still, but they are now somewhat more subtle.

There has been much written in the New Age press about auras, and what great insights they provide about a person's character, health, and so on; with certain colors and shapes meaning certain things. I can't say that I've ever found auras to be all that revealing, so as to be able to decode any person on the spot.

Auras are about as common as noses, and only slightly more interesting.

Oh, those persons who are said to be in radiant health sometimes have auras that are energetic in a particular way. As do people who are fasting. The auras of children who are, say, four to six years of age are often simple, pretty, and well-formed. Elegant. But the auras of most adults are less engaging.

Occasionally, I will see an aura of interest, of striking beauty or hue or intensity, which stands out, just as one might notice a person who is exceptionally good-looking.

Or, occasionally, I will see someone in whom a river flows, as he or she attends to God.

<< 4 >>

The Flow of Sanctity

✶ Father Bertran

WHEN I WAS ATTENDING St. Bonaventure, there were almost a hundred friars in the friary, and all those who were priests (versus brothers) celebrated mass daily. Many of the friars con-celebrated the morning mass.

In addition to the main altar, there were perhaps twenty small altars lining the perimeter of the church, each dedicated to a different saint, where the friars could say their daily office by themselves, a celebration between themselves and their God.

In either case, the masses occurred largely within the Franciscan community.

A couple of masses were held at the friary each Sunday for the general public. Each priest said public masses a couple of times a year, on a rotational schedule.

It was a big deal for these priests to speak publicly. Half a year of attending to God, perhaps; with only a few chances at the public release of the inspired Spirit.

Now, friars come in all shapes and sizes, with all kinds of personal characteristics. When I was at St. Bonaventure, there were severe, old-school friars who had entered the order in the 1940s; and then, there were gentle, scholastic, brainy friars who also had also entered the order in the 1940s. There were good-looking, affable (should I even say cool?) friars who had come into the order in the 1960s, and with whom one might have a beer and talk about things of consequence.

And then there was Father Bertran.

Father Bertran was a tiny man, standing five feet or less and weighing perhaps 110 pounds. The brown robe he wore seemed to be too big for him, which was probably the smallest that was made. He was middle-aged, round-faced, and wore glasses.

If you said hello to him, he would always respond with a big, hearty "Good Morning!"—a greeting intended, I'm sure, to compensate for his size. But if you talked to him further, his voice would drop, and he would look away. His words came with difficulty. He was shy, self-conscious.

Sometimes you would find him in the morning wandering around campus with his camera—an old, old camera in a leather case, beetle brown—taking pictures of God knows what.

At any rate, it was Father Bertran who was saying public mass that morning. I didn't notice anything special about his aura until he started his homily.

He began with a few prepared notes, then started to talk about the Spirit. His words faltered, came hesitantly, and he looked up, as if for divine guidance, and continued talking, and an eloquent line stumbled forward, and then another, and another . . .

And as he spoke, his aura grew, intensified until I could barely see the man for it.

White-purple, flowing, ten feet tall.

When he finished his homily, his aura dropped back to something approaching normal, and he continued to celebrate mass. It stayed that way until he began to consecrate the bread and wine. Again his aura grew, purple-white fire behind the altar.

I would not be surprised if other people at mass, if cued to the event, might also have seen a light around Father Bertran, so dramatic was it. But there was no sign of recognition on any other person's part.

I learned several things from this occurrence.

First, I learned that it is very hard, if not impossible, to accurately assess or predict any individual's spirituality based on his or her public persona.

I also learned something about the Spirit, and about sanctity. I had witnessed a moment of sanctity moving through Father Bertran. But whenever I saw him after that, over a period of years, his aura was quite normal.

Sanctity was a visitor. Something that comes by grace, not as something possessed.

The most one can hope for in this life is to offer freely an opportunity for sanctity to manifest itself.

The rest is not our business.

✳ Certain Questions

WE TEND TO THINK of people whom we believe to be holy, as in some sense transformed.

People fundamentally different from ourselves.

We tend to put some great distance between us and those whom we feel are holy. Impute an excellence to the supposed holy person. Put the person on a pedestal.

And so let me ask you (if you were to believe me): Do you believe Father Bertran to be holy?

There are very few religious or spiritual people who do not recall a personal moment of sanctity. A moment of grace. A freighted moment, in which one was able to give or receive help, to say or be told exactly the right thing, at exactly the right moment.

A moment of insight and inspired action that resolved, perfectly, in an unanticipated way, a host of agonizing issues.

A moment in which one knew that one had witnessed the action of God's grace within the world.

If you are one of those people who have had an experience of God's grace, do you believe yourself to be holy?

Do you think you earned such grace, or that that grace came to you in spite of yourself?

Do you believe Father Bertran earned such grace?

✸ No Reason in Particular

THE FIRST PERSON I MET who had had a mystical experience similar to my own was my theology professor. He had had his experience as a Trappist monk, a life he had lived for six years, followed by a year when he lived as a religious hermit. Interestingly, as a Camaldolese hermit, he chafed at the "insufficient isolation" of the hermitage.

Ultimately, he left the religious life, earned his doctorate, got married, and had a couple of kids; and he was then teaching theology at St. Bonaventure when I met him.

He was telling me once of his novitiate in the monastery, and his first years there; and I commented that he must certainly have fallen into a certain spiritual groove, a pattern of great peace, great sanctity.

He told me: "I remember a particular day very clearly. It was my second or third year in the monastery, and we were all singing the mass, several rows deep, and I must confess, it was all I could do to prevent myself from reaching out and strangling the brother in the row below me!"

"Why did you want to strangle him?" I asked, surprised.

He thought about it for a moment and said, "Oh, I don't know. No reason in particular . . . "

And yet, this was a man who ultimately became lost in the glory of God.

I am reminded of Padre Pio, a stigmatic and recently declared saint within the Catholic Church, a man of many miracles, who when asked whether he was a saint, responded that he was, in fact, one of the world's greatest sinners.

I don't think he was being modest. I think he meant it.

That Yankee spirituality again.

When the heights sing to us, a reply is invariably heard from the depths, I'm afraid.

✳ The Light Comes from Beyond Yourself

I TEND TO THINK that sanctity, or holiness, is not acquired as other personal attributes are acquired.

It's not a skill. Not a technique. Won't come by your wanting it to come.

One does not become holy by assuming the characteristics of holiness, although the world is filled with people who deceive themselves and others by their mimicry.

Sanctity is not something acquired in the way that other attributes are acquired. Rather, it comes by providing less resistance to the Infinite. To reduce what in yourself covers the light; to eliminate, as best you can, what blocks it. To offer, as best you can, your hospitality.

The light comes from beyond your self, and if it comes, it comes as a gift.

You cannot create it, but you can impede it.

❋ A Direct Effect

AS I LISTENED to Father Bertran, I found his words moving beyond the words actually spoken.

Clearly, he was a man of no great rhetorical flourish. Perhaps I was simply impressed by his aura? Well, no doubt I was, but I think that something more than that was going on.

Now, Father Bertran, I'm sure, knew nothing about chakras in those years (if now) and needed no such knowledge after all. His religious education was a Catholic religious education, and any esoteric understanding he possessed was based upon Catholic monasticism.

Watching him say mass that day, I did see that he knew a great deal about poverty of spirit.

How happy are the poor in spirit! Theirs is the kingdom of God!

And just who are the poor in spirit?

Those people who are not so full of themselves that they know a certain inner emptiness. Who, when attentive to God, might have the space to have a river run through them. And there was certainly something running through Father Bertran that day.

When people have this river running through them, they radiate. And when they radiate, they can affect people directly. Can transmit something of their own spiritual state to other people in sympathy with them, through that radiation.

How many of those at mass were in sympathy with Father Bertran that day? Only God knows.

Whatever their number, I suspect that they were far outnumbered by those who had their minds set on what they would have that afternoon for dinner; or by those who felt themselves to be suffering through a mass said by a small, awkward man who seemed to have trouble getting his words out.

✳ Various Dimensions of Religious Leaders

CONGREGATIONS OF religious and spiritual people around the world are generally led by a class of people whose function it is to lead them. Priests. Reverends. Rabbis. Gurus. Mullahs.

And these leaders have many potential, functional dimensions.

Part of their function is to offer commonsense guidance in matters of overall human relations, so that spouses do not act like idiots toward each other or their children, and vice versa. To encourage a certain harmony within the community served and the overall community at large.

Although such leadership is usually positive, I hesitate to call it spiritual, even though it is often conducted in a religious or spiritual setting. It is that a certain interpersonal peace is required before more profound matters can be entered into; and a great deal of time is spent in almost all congregations getting the group to "settle."

Once (and if) this can be achieved, the competent leader can then turn to more spiritual matters. The leaders of a community are generally more knowledgeable about both the group's traditions and the process of teaching; and once they have achieved a social harmony, they attempt to pass on the spiritual wisdom ceded their religion. A good preacher, of whatever denomination or dogma, brings insight to his or her congregation. Inspires the faithful. Delivers a certain *Aha!* to the community, which opens them further to the richness of their tradition and the meaning of their lives. Clearly, this is a spiritual function, in that the people's awarenesses becomes larger, fuller than they were prior to their leaders' ministrations.

❀ The Transmission of Spiritual States

IN SOME GROUPS and congregations, there is the possibility of transmission of spiritual states, from the few to the many.

In such cases, the leader of the group, or even someone else in the group, has attained a certain spiritual state, a certain relationship with the divine, in which a spirit radiates. Then the group harmonizes itself in accordance with this radiated spirit, which promulgates itself broadly across the community.

This type of relationship with the divine is difficult to pass on in any other way than from person to person. Or perhaps poetry to person.

* * *

I happen to belong to a parish that is known throughout the area as a "good" parish. A parish that has a certain spirit that has been rumbling along for decades, unchanged by the coming and going of its many parishioners, the coming and going of its many priests. A spirit, apparently, not lightly surrendered. A spirit that has taken hold in a community, apart from the individuals who constitute it.

This knowledge of the transmittability of spiritual states is, of course, widely known among all the world's religions. In Christianity, there is the transmission of the Holy Spirit, which happens for the Catholic at Confirmation. Among Zen students, there is the dharma transmission. During *bayat*, or initiation, the Sufi delivers a transmission to his student that he believes originates with Mohammed. An aspirant to Kriya yoga receives Shaktipat, a transmission that awakens the person's chakras and points him or her to God.

Many of these transmissions occur at points of initiation, as part of an outer ceremony. They may or may not be effective, depending on the relationship of the transmitter with God, and the capacity of the transmittee to recognize the transmission, resonate with the transmission, and make use of it.

✳ Not All Spirits Come from God

IT SHOULD BE NOTED, of course, that not all supposedly religious or spiritual groups that are harmonized, have harmonized themselves around the spirit. Many cults and cult-groups have become self-harmonized by methods far more Machiavellian than a shared spirit.

One should not abandon one's common sense in the process of becoming a member of any community.

I have always tried (for example) to avoid groups that maintain stores of poisons, incendiaries, and weapons. Particularly the ones that believe that a looming firefight with some opposing, demonized party is somehow destined to cause the onset of the Apocalypse; as well as those who believe themselves to be slated for imminent, metaphysical triumph.

As the Bible warns, not all spirits come from God.

There are many groups that have some manner of spiritual agency manifestly flowing through them, but that are, in other ways, well . . . certifiably nuts.

People tend to want things to be cleanly one way or the other, and so conclude either that some group which seems to have some aspect of the spiritual at work in it can't be nuts; or, conversely, that if it's nuts, it can't have some spiritual agency at work in it.

I'm afraid they're wrong on both counts.

I mean, look at the Mormons.

✳

✳ Oh Ye Mormons!

I'M JUST joshing you.

Anything for a laugh!

For I am a nut also, and one of you.

My Unitarian friend thinks that I am a nut for being a kind-of-Catholic. A nut for being satisfactorily, spiritually led by a bunch of sexually-confused old men in robes.

My Evangelical co-worker thinks my Unitarian friend is a nut. A person so liberal, he'd give his own job to a lesbian of color, if only she'd ask.

Why won't she ask?

My wife's uncle, who is a Texan and who goes to church where the ushers are armed, and who thinks that we are aged thirty-three in the resurrection, because Jesus was thirty-three when he died, is, well . . . a nut.

And unlike me, my Unitarian friend, my Evangelical co-worker, and ninety-seven percent of Mormons, he really is a nut. Mad as a freakin' hatter.

Some people really are.

You got to draw a line somewhere.

Like weaponry.

✳

❋ It's the Laugh

SPEAKING OF NUTS, in the years that followed my experience of God, I noted that a very peculiar sort of transmission from myself to others periodically occurred.

Father Bertrand radiated from the altar; whereas I, I seemed to radiate sometimes when I really laughed.

Yeah, laughed.

(If this was really [as we Catholics say] a charism, then it is proof positive that God has a sense of humor. What a practical joke, on me! What a freakin' charism!)

Before the experience, I don't recall ever having had a good belly laugh. Since the experience, I've had such laughs. And the laugh sometimes seems to have an unusual effect on others. This happened a handful of times per year, for several connected years, especially in the years following the experience.

As an example, I was once in a restaurant with a friend who was making some kind of joke, and I was really laughing. Out of the corner of my eye, I saw a man get up from his table, several tables away, and hurry over to ours:

"Make that sound again," he demanded. "Make that sound! Was it a laugh? Laugh again! Incredible laugh." The man stood by our table, looking at me, as though I could issue it at will.

This sort of thing has happened many times with many variants. Not often, but with a certain regularity over a period of years.

Earlier I wrote:

And as I sought to discern how stone could have such a presence, I caught sight of God, the movement of water upon water, who delighted, laughing. Emerged as the Reality of the I am of the stone.

Unimaginably ancient, alive in incomprehensible fullness. And He laughed me.

We laughed together! Like a mirror I was to Him, like a Mirror He to me!

Ever since that day, I have come to believe that humor and spirituality are tightly linked, at least for me. For when I was confronted with God, our response was laughter.

Now, laughter, when you think about it, is the reconciliation of opposites. The recognition of what is really going on, as opposed to what you were led to think was going on. Based on the discovery of the Truth.

Almost every bit of humor is based on a comparison of what is really going on with what one thought was going on. Every laugh.

Need an example? Think of any joke.

An American tourist went into a provincial Spanish town for dinner one evening, and after going into a fine restaurant on the plaza, he asked to be served the specialty of the house. After the meal arrived, the man asked what sort of meat it contained. "Sir," said the waiter, "those are the cajones." "The what you say!" exclaimed the tourist. "They are, how you say, the testicles of the bull that was killed in the ring today," explained the waiter. The tourist did not want to offend the waiter, and so tasted the dish and found it to be truly delicious. Returning the following day, he asked for the same meal. After finishing the meal, the tourist commented to the waiter: "Today's cajones were much smaller than the ones I had yesterday." "True sir," said the waiter, ". . . you see, the bull, he does not always lose."

Humor is based on the tension between what is expected and

what is real. Which is why my experience of God was filled with laughter:

My expectations of Him, and His Reality!

I can only conclude that others have had a sudden, compelling sense of Him in the echo of that laugh.

❀ Truth, Love, and Beauty Are Experiences of God

Beauty is truth, truth beauty—that is all
Ye know on earth, and all ye need to know.
                                        —*John Keats*

IN THE YEARS following my experience of God, I became convinced that the experience of truth, beauty, and love are all experiences of God.

During those years, the presence of God was often overpowering; and as His presence would increase (as I have mentioned) my consciousness would increase, and time would start to slow. This same sort of effect occurred when I experienced beauty, especially spiritual beauty. Or when I felt a welling up of love. Or when, in class or otherwise, I was struck by something profoundly true. Reality would intensify in a wave.

My experience of God began with my contemplation of one of the most beautiful scenes I had ever witnessed, which subsequently led to insights into my own nature, the nature of God, and the nature of the world.

An experience of beauty that was converted into an experience of love, an experience of truth.

I have spoken to you about how my senses were unified during my experience of God. How sight, hearing, and taste were unified. How the gaps between them were filled in by heretofore unknown modes of sensing, which proceeded through the surfaces of things.

In an analogous way, I knew that what we experience as beauty, love, and truth are in fact part of the continuum of God, the recognition of God by disparate means.

In my discussion of the chakras, I noted how each of the chakras reflects a different aspect of consciousness, using a different sort of vocabulary. That the mind thinks in the vocabulary of thought, the heart "thinks" in the vocabulary of feeling, and the genitals "think" in the vocabulary of sexuality. That these and the other chakras each has a perspective into the Infinite; and that when discovering the Infinite, is called by different names: Truth, Beauty, and Love.

And so I concluded that what the mind experiences when it realizes the truth of something is in fact the experience of God.

And that when the heart has real love of someone, it is an experience of God.

And wherever beauty is experienced—whether the head, the heart, or somewhere else—it also is an experience of God.

❊ God as a Faceted Being

THE HUMAN EXPERIENCE OF GOD is in some sense like that of a faceted jewel that reflects light in many directions but has one center, one source. All these experiences—the experience of love, beauty, or truth—have a certain *Aha!* to them. An understanding that one has touched something significant. Something real.

When an engineer is trying to figure out where a given radio station is transmitting from, he or she takes many directional readings from widely separated places and traces each reading, called a line of bearing, onto a map. Where those lines intersect is the location of the transmitter. This process is called triangulation.

Given that our experience of God is a faceted thing, it is important to try to triangulate Him.

The Sufi orders all have a practice known as *dhikr* or *ẓikr*, which is done like prayer, both personally and as part of a community. It is similar to, but with some significant differences from, the Hindu use of mantras.

As part of Islamic tradition, God is said to have ninety-nine names. These names include The Truth, The Source, The Forgiver, The Majestic, The Sincere, The Provider.

As part of *dhikr*, some subset of these names is recited, either aloud or to oneself, and may be accompanied by the repetition of certain prayers. Sometimes these words and prayers may be repeated tens of thousands of times.

Each name is considered to have a specific effect on one's spirituality; and often it is one's spiritual director who prescribes the repetition of a particular name, or group of names, to the novice. This allows the person to focus on one aspect of God for long periods of time, until it makes its mark.

As the various names have different "flavors," there is also an aspect of triangulating God through this practice.

And as the person goes through a process much like that described by Patanjali, God is more fully revealed, and His presence arises from that revelation, and in that presence, an ecstasy arises.

For to be alone with God is bliss.

✻ Love Has No Flutter

LET ME DISCUSS God as love for a moment.

Perhaps if we invert the terms, as my seventh-grade algebra assures me I can do, it might shake off some of the sense of platitude that the statement bears.

Let me, therefore, discuss love as God.

In what sense is Love God? Is it simply that love is one of God's attributes? That God loves us?

I think the answer is more surprising than that. To see what I mean, think of someone you love and pay close attention to the feeling of love. Try to locate the source of this love within yourself, where this love is coming from. Find that exact spot, and you may be surprised.

Contemplate That.

It is Silent. Unmoving. Cocksure. Bright.

There are so many rhythms that play about us, play through us. The rhythm of the heart. The rhythm of the breath. The hum of power through the wires. The turn of wheels.

Love has no hum. Love has no rhythm. No periodicity. No flutter.

Love doesn't even seem to flutter with death. It is absolutely unchanged. And what is unchanged? What is it that is indifferent even to death?

Who do you think?

We are all of us mystics, when we love, for God is playing through us.

✿ *Aha!*

AND WE ARE MYSTICS as well when we understand the roots of truth and beauty.

The *Aha!* we experience when we recognize truth is joy at finding the Real!

It is the *Aha!* that interests me, that thing that leaps inside us when confronted with truth. It is our compass. It is our gauge. That with which we meter truth.

What is it that we are metering when we measure Truth?

* * *

And then beauty. What is our response to beauty? Beauty that stops us in our tracks.

What is it that stops us in our tracks?

Someone might argue that people all over the world get that *Aha!* feeling all the time, thinking that they have figured something out; only to have that realization turn out to be wildly off-base. And I suppose, factually, that observation is correct.

In response, I might offer a quote from William Blake, that: "Every thing possible to be believ'd is an image of the truth."

Note that Blake says that it is an "image" of the truth, rather than the truth itself.

In this world, there is no absolute truth; St. Paul reminds us that in this world, we see through a glass darkly. What we know about the world is always tainted by our knowledge's approximate, or incomplete nature; and therefore what we know as truth is always, unavoidably commingled with falsity. Even those mathematical or scientific facts that we believe to be absolutely true suffer in the same sense that the three dimensional world, when rendered in two dimensions, loses something important, no matter how cleverly it is rendered.

Given this, even our errors in judgment can be said to have had some true aspects within that error. To find an image of the truth even within the factually false.

❋ The Sufi Sense of Heart

IN THOSE YEARS following my effacement in God, when I would be confronted with the beautiful, or the true, or love, my consciousness of God would instantly deepen, and time would slow down.

In some sense, each of these provocations would have a somewhat different effect on the same bit of inner real estate that was connected with the knowledge of God's presence. I noted that truth was determined by the mind, certainly, but also by the heart. And love, though primarily a thing of the heart, might also evoke some sense of the sexual, depending on the person associated with love's arising. And beauty, while arriving through the senses and being validated by the heart, was also engaged by the mind.

The Sufis give much importance to the heart, or *qalb*, a heart distinct from that physical, beating organ. Not only is the heart the place where we find God indwelling in love, but it is also where we recognize many other sorts of things as well.

When we in the West think of something "tugging at the heart" or of someone "having a troubled heart," we tend to define the operation of the heart in terms of rather gross sensations. Often what tugs at the heart is something that is simply the overly-sentimental. That which troubles the heart might be anger, or guilt, or worry. We have fairly coarse words to discuss things of the heart: love, anger, joy, sadness, loss. We tend not only to have coarse emotions, but also to have those emotions in a violent way.

✺ The Sacred and Immaculate Hearts

AS A CATHOLIC, I grew up with images of Jesus in which he pointed toward his sacred heart, a visible heart wrapped by an aura, or fire.

Similarly, images of the Virgin Mary sometimes display her immaculate heart, also wreathed with fire.

My local church, built in the late 1890s, has facing stained glass windows of both Jesus and Mary with their hearts aflame, as have many older Catholic churches.

The images of the hearts of Jesus and Mary indicate that their hearts are pure, that they are spontaneously filled with compassion for suffering, and also delight in the things that delight God. But these images also suggest that their hearts are open to that finely articulated, direct knowing of which the heart is capable. So dramatic a capacity that it needs to be portrayed as part of their physical representation, Jesus pointing to his visible, subtle heart.

For the Sufis, the opening and the conscious employment of the faculty of the heart is a key achievement in the spiritual journey, an achievement that makes the next stages of growth possible.

There is a hadith in Islam, in which God says, "Neither My heavens nor My earth contain Me, but the heart of My faithful believer contains Me."

It is only the heart, as that faculty of spiritual perception, which has the ability to hold God as He is.

If you look to that imperishable thing that rests at the base of the heart, under Love, you may find Him there.

❋ Spiritual Virtues

THE SEARCH for that which underlies the heart must begin, for many people, with the cultivation of certain spiritual virtues; and it is unfortunate that so many people fundamentally misunderstand these spiritual virtues.

They think of them as personal accomplishments, rather than as tools, and this attitude is disabling.

Take humility, for example. Humility is considered to be a virtue in almost every religion. Why is that? Is it because God likes the humble and will reward them therefore for their humility? Give them a gold star in the Book of Life? Because they have met that rigorous standard of praiseworthy behavior?

God does not grade our conduct as a Sunday school teacher might.

The point of manifesting humility is to allow room for God to act in us.

How happy are the poor in spirit! Theirs is the kingdom of God!

And why are the poor in spirit happy?

I mentioned that Father Bertran knew poverty of spirit, and therefore had the room to have God move through him. A space within Bertran through which God might act.

Humility is a nearly empty cup waiting to be filled. The full cup can, after all, tolerate no more.

Humility is a requirement for God's intervention, giving Him room to maneuver. It offers to God hospitality—the invitation and the room for God to make Himself manifest.

This is not a matter of gold stars. Humility is not a virtue that

God fawns over; but rather is a practical precondition for access to Him. It is a necessary element, like flour is to bread.

There is an active point to humility, like a motor in a car. It doesn't exist for its own sake.

❦ Attention to God

WHAT ABOUT paying attention to God?

Must we pay attention to God because He gets offended if we don't? He gets in a snit?

Or worse, He's like some egomaniacal Hollywood type, who will sulk or lash out at an inattentive member of His entourage? If we don't spend enough time sucking up? If we seem to forget who's boss?

Many of the people who attend church on Sunday, or temple or mosque on Friday, act as if they think this way; and are simply there paying their dues. Sort of like paying the electric bill.

Well, at least they show up, I suppose.

And that, I suppose, is the point. That at a bare minimum, people will at least give a little thought to God each week. Because the thought of God changes us.

Like humility and patience, attentiveness to God is a key component of the spiritual process. It is important because it has an important effect, not because it's part of the grading criteria. Attention to God has practical consequences on our spiritual direction and our spiritual ability, and on the grace with which we conduct our lives.

God gives out neither number nor letter grades. No gold stars. But He cannot help but notice . . . that you can dance.

* * *

What important effect does attentiveness to God have, if not on His good graces?

As I have said, the thought of God changes us.

As I wrote a while back, a river must have direction, or else it is a swamp. Growth also must have direction; or it pools, and turns stagnant.

As George Harrison says, "If you don't know where you're going / any road will take you there."

God gives you someplace to head toward.

And as you head toward the Infinite, you will have plenty of room into which to grow, won't you?

Room to grow, room to play. Room for the children of God to romp in.

I have written a little bit about mind-poise, which is the act of concentrating on one thing, thinking thoroughly upon it, getting perspective on it from many angles, and then at last, holding it in contemplation.

And I have also written that once one's contemplation has been successful, one achieves an intuitive knowledge about the matter pursued.

And I have said that God is a bigger God than is contained in our Bible and Qur'an and Vedas, and may be approached, in addition to religion, by science, by art, by friends, by a walk in the country. That God must be triangulated. That ways of thinking about God are limited only by one's imagination.

As one is attentive to God over a period of years, in an ever-growing way, one undergoes a process that is very much like mind-poise.

For as one contemplates God, well . . . the penny may just drop.

And God will lead you from there.

✸ God Will Lead You from There

HOW DOES GOD LEAD one from there?

The thought of God changes us. And the presence of God, which is a stage beyond mere thought of Him, changes us still further.

It is by the direction of those changes that we are led.

Led as we are by those changes, our decisions are always still our own. Even God's presence gives us no road map other than our reoriented character.

But help we have. For if one makes decisions in God's presence, one makes very different decisions than those made without His presence.

No supernatural special effects are needed for God to have His say.

⊰ 5 ⊱

Spiritual Vanity

✺ Various Sorts of Arrogance

IN THE YEARS THAT FOLLOWED my experience of God, I spoke about it to a couple of Franciscan friars.

They had no similar experiences to answer with. In my own spiritual competition, I was 15-love. Perhaps even match-over.

And given this, I assumed that I enjoyed a uniquely superior spiritual status to theirs.

Well, not exactly unique. But a brotherhood shared by Jesus and the Buddha and Mohammed and the saints, and me.

That I, though afraid of the full effect of God, was wiser than those ordinary friars in matters of the spirit.

And although I said nothing like this, this is what I thought.

That I was wiser in the spirit than those who had given their lives over to God.

Imagine the arrogance.

I happened to attend a college reunion recently, and as part of the reunion weekend, I went to a lecture by Father Gervase (who has since passed on), who spoke about Thomas Merton, the famous Catholic mystic who lived, for a time, at St. Bonaventure.

Over the course of his presentation, which lasted for an hour or so, I saw on display a subtler understanding than I now possess, about Merton and matters of the spirit. A refinement I can only hope to attain.

And yet Father Gervase, I know, had had no experience like my own.

His spiritual stature reflected a patient and prayerful life in the spirit, filled with many luminous moments. Apparently, whether the penny falls, or the dime, nickel, or half-dollar, what counts is the worth of what's in the basket.

Not the size of the coin.

✻ Wrestling the Ego

ALL AND ALL, I wish I could report that my coming face-to-face with God had killed my ego and that all that remained was a puddle of sentient goo; which has, kindly, remained on earth for the benefit of such as you, the reader.

If only that were the case!

Although this coming face-to-face instantly and dramatically altered me, my ego healed up quite nicely, thank you. I've met three other people who have had experiences similar to my own, and none of them would deny the existence of their ego. To the contrary, they are quick to make fun of it! I and these people will tell you that it is the wrestling with the ego that gives people their spiritual muscle. You have to recognize your ego before you can wrestle with it; and unfortunately most people cannot differentiate between it and their true Self.

I have met many supposedly "spiritual" people over the course of my life, some of them quite well-known; and while some are quite genuine, many are not. I must confess that I believe myself to be better than average at seeing these people's reality. And I would offer you this piece of advice: if anyone tells you that he or she has no ego, run.

Run.

Those people I believe are truly spiritual all see through the ego and understand some of its wiles. At best, this allows them to compensate for it when they see it pop up.

But it always plays about us, or worse, plays through us.

The ego is a survivor. It can even survive death.

Ever wonder why that ghost continues to haunt that old house, decade in and decade out?

I suspect that at the root of it all is some spirit, fulminating: This is my house, dammit. Who in hell do those people think they are?

The ego thinks like humans think. When we think like God thinks, the ego submerges, and it plots its return when our guard is down.

When we walk down the street, and smile and nod to some well-dressed man or woman, and avert our eyes from the homeless man standing over a grate, it is the ego's doing. Our ego instinctively implies that we are laudable people who properly respect, and are properly respected by our own kind; and who owe not even the slightest human affirmation to those who are our social inferiors.

God doesn't think like that, thank God.

Sometimes having a religious or spiritual orientation can help weaken the ego, so that we think more often like God. And sometimes a religious orientation can make the ego far worse.

✺ An Ego Run Amok

ONE CAN FIND EXAMPLES in any religion of how a religious orientation can make people's ego far worse, since ego is bound up
with all of our spiritual searches. The problem of an inflated ego
does, however, seem to be much worse in fundamentalisms of all
sorts, whether Christian or Muslim; of the Hindu, or of the Jew.

And I think that the reason this is often the case, is that the fundamentalist form of any religion actively encourages a specific sort
of spiritual vanity.

I know, for example, many fundamentalists of all stripes who feel
that they have it together. They have a fine and attractive spouse,
live in an expensive house, are proud of their children, have an
upstanding life built on hard work and deep faith. They feel that
they are among the elect. Know that they are saved and are among
God's favorites. Have a treasure built up in heaven. And thanks
be to God they are not like those others. Like the mass of humanity who are lost, deceived, deluded, broken. Like those who know
nothing of God or, worse, are actively God's enemies.

They come to believe that they are deservedly part of God's
upper-middle-class, thanks be to God!

Or, if they are devout and poor, they believe their poverty to be
a sacrifice that they are making to be among God's elect, to be
saved, to be among God's favorites, to have a treasure built up
for them in heaven.

The particular life circumstances may change, but the attitude
doesn't: We're very OK. Everyone else who does not share our
beliefs is deluded or worse.

Hard to get more egotistical than that.

It's common for fundamentalists, whether Christian, Muslim, Hindu, or Jew, to believe that the world is set against anyone who lives the true faith.

This allows them to enjoy their special status even more. They believe that they are racking up coinage in some spiritual bank account, a treasure stored for them in heaven.

It never dawns on them that what the world is reacting to is their sanctimonious and arrogant worldview. That rather than being understood as spiritual persons, they are understood, rather, as examples of the ego run amok.

❋ Science Fundamentalism

OF COURSE, one of the most durable and widespread of fundamentalisms in the Western world today is that of Science.

People of science would never, of course, use the word fundamentalist to describe their worldview. A very unscientific term. But like any other group that thinks it has the upper hand on reality, these people have faith in a creed that will not be budged, and a set of premises that cannot be questioned.

Not all scientists are science fundamentalists, of course, but a core group of science literalists may be found behind most major technological or scientific endeavors. One hallmark of this fundamentalism is the insistence that all subject-matters must be subjected to the same fundamental mode of investigation. This mode of investigation tries to use the same wrench for every nut, whatever its size or shape.

For the science fundamentalist, that wrench is the belief that all phenomena are ultimately reducible to known physical properties, which may be tested using the empirical method.

Science fundamentalists prefer the hard sciences. Mathematics. Physics. Chemistry. The macho sciences. Even biology is, well, a little too foo-foo for them.

Psychology? Sociology? Only semi-sciences.

Philosophy? Religion? The arts? Poetry?   Snort.

Even if such things had value (which is an unproven assertion), the value, if any, undoubtedly had its origin somewhere in the hard sciences. The reality behind the hard sciences is the greater reality, the more profound view of the real. More real than the ephemera of such vaporous things, as poetry and the arts.

❧

✴ God Created in the Laboratory

WHICH IS WHY WE GET such studies as "Neuropsychological Bases of God Beliefs."

No kidding.

A few years ago, there were several reports about various scientists who had located an area of the brain that, when subjected to the right experimental conditions, resulted in "the feeling of God-like experiences."

The author of one of these reports, a professor of neuroscience named Michael Persinger, was asked if his work led him to the conclusion that God is solely the creation of brain wave activity. His response:

My point of view is, "Let's measure it. Let's keep an open mind and realize maybe there is no God; maybe there might be. We're not going to answer it by arguments—we're going to answer it by measurement and understanding the areas of the brain that generate the experience and the patterns that experimentally produce it in the laboratory."

So, God as brain artifact, maybe. Which we will discover with further research.

✱ A Zen Story

I AM REMINDED of an old Zen story, translated many years ago by Paul Repp.

Hogen, who was a Chinese Zen teacher, lived alone in a small temple in the country. One day, four traveling monks appeared and asked if they might make a fire in his yard to warm themselves.

While they were building a fire, Hogen heard them arguing about subjectivity and objectivity. He joined them and said, "There is a big stone. Do you consider it to be inside or outside your mind?"

One of the monks replied, "From the Buddhist viewpoint, everything is an objectification of mind, so I would say that the stone is inside my mind."

"Your head must feel very heavy," observed Hogen, "if you are carrying around a stone like that in your mind."

✿ The Hard Sciences

THE HARD-SCIENCES are the rigid bulwark of science fundamentalism.

Hard-science fundamentalists judge their own excellence by the hard standards of science; and their imaginations know no boundaries as to the areas in which they could potentially apply their hard-science skills.

Kind of like a world-class power-weight-lifter who, absolutely confident of his abilities, takes on the lead male role in *Swan Lake*, figuring (after all) that it's nothing he can't handle.

And who is, at best, a pretty ungraceful sight.

And who is, at worse, well: rather pathetic.

❦ Fundamentalists Think the Worst of God

ONE OF MY BIGGEST BEEFS with fundamentalists of all sorts is that they tend to think the worst of God.

The God of the hard-sciences, for example, is limited to that insensate jumble that the physical universe comprises. The science fundamentalists believe that all we have acquired, as persons, through sense, pain, and struggle, is flushed into oblivion upon death; our only persistence through our atomic elements, dispersed.

And then there are those religious fundamentalists, the ones who think that God is out to fry a significant percentage of the world's population; especially those who do not share their religious, or increasingly, political convictions.

A God with a mean streak as wide as the white on a skunk's back.

It seems to me that the scientists don't seem to understand that the universe is more than the summation of mass, force, and natural law. They don't seem to understand that there is a powerful intellect at work in the universe; and that this intellect knows Itself and is woven into us at many, many levels beyond the physical.

Many religious fundamentalists seem to think that God has room in His heart only for those they admire. Only for those they consider truly worthy of His love.

But God is more excellent than our conceits of Him.

A few hundred years ago, the mass of humankind thought that all that was in the universe was the flat planet earth and a bunch of pinpricks of light in the sky. The sun and the moon.

Heaven. And Hell.

And that was it.

Now, we point the Hubble space telescope at some distant, postage stamp of sky and find within it galaxy upon galaxy upon galaxy. And a trillion stars in each galaxy, with trillions of potential planets around those stars.

When we look downward, within the atom, we find ever-finer particles. Our universe is expanding downward as rapidly as it is upward. It wasn't much more than a hundred years ago that mankind thought that the atom was the ultimate small bit of matter.

Over the last few hundred years, our understanding of the magnitude of what exists has grown explosively; and grows explosively wherever we look. All we have to do is look, and there is more there than we possibly could have imagined.

More more.

There is always more more.

More mercy than we can possibly imagine. More fun.

✳ Liquid Arrogance

SPEAKING OF SCIENCE AND MERCY, the other night I had a couple of beers and wrote a letter to Stephen Hawking, the famous physicist. That guy in the wheelchair, with a fragile toehold in this dimension, whose center of mass is in the abstract, pulsating, electro-magnetical Other.

I went on and on.

Something about there being no dark matter, just existent dimensions other than this one, which are not accounted for, but nonetheless cause observed gravitational effects.

And how physics could never determine the root of nonlocal events without introducing consciousness as a variable, since it is a fundamental property of nature.

And how the human being is a fractal of all that is, and so one may, in some sense, study man to discover more about even the distant aspects of the universe.

And how consciousness and time are inversely related, and how it would be interesting to know more about consciousness via the mathematics generated from its inclusion in the equations that describe the physical world.

That kind of stuff.

Crank stuff.

Funny what beer will do.

Gives one the courage to advise people like Stephen Hawking on subjects like Physics that one last studied in high school, long ago, and for which one earned a D+.

Dr. Hawking, if you read this, I just wanted to say that I will not be disappointed if you fail to answer my letter.

And also . . . please excuse the handwriting.

⊷ 6 ⊶

Dimensions of
Guidance

❋ I Hate to Complain, But . . .

GOD HAS BEEN SO VERY KIND TO ME in so many ways that I hate to complain.

But throughout my life, God has left me pretty much out at sea.

I mean, it's one thing to not know He's there, and then not get direction from Him. You kind of expect to not get direction from someone you don't know is there. But not getting direction from Someone you know is there, and could help if He wanted to; well, that kind of pisses you off.

You might have noticed in the story about my effacement in God that no hierarchies stood between God and myself. I would have preferred, all things being equal, to have encountered Jesus, or Mary, or Mohammed, or the Buddha, or the archangel Gabriel, or the archangel Michael, or Moses, or Saint Swithin. Any sort of arbiter; any someone to whom I could look for direction.

But sorry. It didn't happen like that.

If it had happened like that, I might have had a clue as to what to do next.

If it had been Mohammed or Rumi, I could have converted to Islam. If Moses, I could have become a Jew, if they'd have me. If Jesus or Mary or Saint Swithin, I could have become a priest, a monk, or a Christian religious hermit. If my experience had been of a person, some lesser being than God, perhaps he or she would have let something drop. Given me a hint.

But no hint was given.

Not that God doesn't do that sort of thing. But He certainly didn't with me.

✸ Direction from God

SAINT FRANCIS WAS TOLD to rebuild a church. Now that's what I call direction. Saint Paul was told whom to visit in order to recover his sight, once he had been knocked off his ass.

That's direction.

Based on my experience alone, I could have as easily been a Hindu, Pagan, Muslim, or Jew. I could have been a Buddhist, since I understand their Void to be the Godhead. I could have been any of these things, or none of them.

I considered, at several points, becoming a Catholic monk or taking religious orders of some sort. A Benedictine. A priest. A religious hermit. But two things held me back.

The first was that a monastic life is a very regimented life, and I have always tried to spit the bit on whatever was constraining me. Unfortunately, I am not disciplined enough for that life; although I sometime wonder who I would have become if I had subjected myself to that discipline.

The second reason had to do with the presence of God.

My sense of the presence of God was very intense, a Great Weight hanging slightly aside my consciousness. I endured a certain awe of God, fear of God, so existentially close was He. And I asked myself, if God was so obtrusive to me as a student—taking classes, going to keg parties—what would happen to me in a monastery? My ego led me to fear that I would disappear entirely.

Oh, yeah. There were also girls.

Not that I was ever particularly good with them, mind you. But I always very much wanted to be. Even still.

✷ Nut or Saint?

AS I'VE DISCUSSED, when I first had my experience, I didn't tell anyone about it for some time, since even I didn't know what to think of it. When I did talk to a few people about it, the results of the conversations were often very different from what I expected. In many cases, no useful thing resulted from my tale, but the people who heard my story treated me differently, fixing me somewhere along that complicated spectrum from saint to nut.

I always deeply hoped that my story would be found useful. But it was seldom taken as something of use, except by those few individuals who were already percolating.

So it was pretty clear to me, thirty years ago, that I was not going to do much that was useful by simply retelling my story. Perhaps in some way I could teach about it?

Perhaps I should be a teacher. A spiritual teacher.

Hmm.

❋ Long Walks in Inclement Weather

IF I HAD SOMEHOW STUMBLED onto some discipline or practice that had led to my effacement, I could have taught that discipline or practice. As a life mission.

But rather than the product of some discipline, I had had the experience while standing in the wind and rain transfixed. What exactly could I teach?

What behavior could I prescribe for my students? Long walks alone in inclement weather, punctuated by long periods of staring at the horizon?

I had not then thought about the heart, and mind-poise for thirty-some years.

So I concluded back then that it made little sense to talk about the matter and that I had nothing particularly useful to teach.

I felt as if I had a thousand-dollar bill that no one could break.

✳ My Dearest Wish

ALTHOUGH GOD HAS BEEN in many ways very good to me, He has given me no road map of what do with either my first experience or my subsequent experiences, which intertwine in some strange dance that has been put in motion, by some distant music.

I was neither a fit monk nor someone who could discuss his interior life without raising suspicions of one sort or another.

I hope I'm discussing the experience better now. I hope thirty years have taught me something.

But I also hope that I have not been inactive for thirty years, and I dearly hope that I was able to do some good, in some unobserved way. Unobserved below people's recognition of the act and the effect.

Some good that freed, a little, my friends, and family, and coworkers. And gave them a little hope. A little courage.

This is my dearest wish, my deepest prayer.

✸ Hidden Service

I HAVE FOR YEARS been an admirer of the works of Idries Shah, who would sometimes tell a story like this story of hidden service:

Bey Ganah would often give his books away, saying to people: "I'm done with these. Would you like to take them?"

Sometimes he would give away his food and clothing as well to people, saying: "I've already eaten! Have the extra! And take that old jacket if you like, I'm too fat to wear it!"

A friend of his, watching this occur over the years, said to him: "People never understand what you're doing for them, and don't have the least indication of what it is costing you. Why don't you at least let them know what you're doing for them so that they show you some appreciation? Because they're getting it for free, they don't think anything much about it."

"I don't want their appreciation," said Bey Ganah. "I just wish to help them. That's enough."

Bey Ganah used to give his teachings in the same way. People had little clue that they were being taught, but being taught they were.

Over the long years, the friends and neighbors of Bey Ganah became known for their wisdom and deep perception, and people came from far and wide to seek their advice and blessing.

Many of the most spiritual people I have encountered throughout my life have not been recognized as spiritual teachers. But teach they did, in a way that went unobserved.

Often, they have not had reputations as particularly spiritual people; or even reputations as good people.

The reason for this is that such people often act like a mirror to the people around them.

They are sufficiently perceptive to discern the limitations in people's ways of being, and to mirror back to them a caricature of their own behavior. And to the vain, they will say something or do something so exquisitely vain that it shocks the person to whom the action mirrors.

Or they will say, to a hateful person who is riddled with prejudice, something so shocking, so specious, so alarmingly prejudiced that the person recoils and has a chance to appreciate, for a moment, what is lurking in his or her own heart.

These things are done without sarcasm, with no hint that they do not actually reflect the teacher's own state.

And so these teachers often acquire reputations that are unsavory, and are not understood to be teachers at all, except as bad examples.

✵ The Spiritual Teacher as Someone Else

ALSO COMMON is the spiritual teacher who is in fact understood to be teaching something else.

English literature, or physics, or tae kwon do, some subject that is cunningly intertwined with a certain spiritual understanding, so that it fuses together in such a manner that the student is broadened in ways that he or she barely understands, via the study of something else.

Such teachers are often understood to have been very good teachers. Years later, their former students still remark, "One of the best courses I ever took was English lit . . . " And then their voices trail off, as if they are trying to recall why a simple English lit course has, over the years, meant so very much to them.

✸ Hidden Masters

IN SOME SUPPOSEDLY SPIRITUAL circles, there is much talk about the existence of "hidden masters," and the individuals (and groups) who make much of these "masters" spend an inordinate amount of time trying to decipher who they are and how they may be contacted. These individuals imagine these "illuminati" to be a kind of cross between a Jedi knight and a medieval alchemist.

They are never able to locate such people, at least not bona fide ones, which is just as well.

Were they to discover that that doddering old English professor down the block . . . that one who dons a pith helmet sort of affair, complete with hanging bee netting, to spray the morning roses . . . that such a one was indeed a "hidden master," their letdown would register 8.2 on the Richter scale.

Similarly, there are legions of seekers who demand that their spiritual teachers call themselves spiritual teachers.

And these people often demand that their teachers have a certain name recognition among *those in the know*. And it doesn't hurt, of course, if a teacher has, by either birth or affectation, an Indian or Tibetan or Arab name, and represents some exotic-sounding organization: Hakuin McBain of the Clear Mountain Zendo Monastery, for example.

Certainly, it is much more impressive to report that one has spent the weekend doing zazen under the tutelage of Hakuin McBain than it is to report that one has spent several hours on a neighbor's patio, drinking lemonade, talking and listening to some doddering old English professor.

And it certainly explains why many wise people teach in ways that go almost unnoticed, and are able thereby to avoid turning their own lives, and the lives of those they teach, into a circus.

✤ White-Hot Pain

OVER THE PAST FEW YEARS, I have somewhat overcome my
reluctance to talk more openly about spiritual matters. I have also
started to receive inquiries from diverse acquaintances, and their
friends, via letter and email, which I have tried to answer as best
I can.

Many of these inquiries, though coming from very different people from around the globe, have common elements that surface
again, and again, and again.

Most of the messages sent me have been quite genuine, written by
people who are obviously thoughtful and decent souls, and who
are motivated to write me out of some level of spiritual pain.

And as someone who has experienced, at points, a white-hot pain
of my own, such entreaties are hard to ignore.

Among the most common messages I receive are those from people who have been very diligent to the point of obsession about
their spiritual studies, and have worked themselves up into an
almost panicked state about their supposed "lack of attainment."

These inquiries frequently contain a long bibliography of the
works they have read, often in the past year or two, including dozens of books from all manner of points of view. And the implicit
question that I am asked is: *Why has the reading of all these books,
which I have pursued with such great earnestness, done my spiritual
state no appreciable good?*

I try to help them as best I can.

✳ Spirituality as Hard Work

SUCH PEOPLE TEND TO HAVE two or three issues going on concurrently, and all must be addressed in order for them to get
better.

Their typical list of books includes a variety of relatively light-
weight, popular titles, among which are mixed some very dense,
very tightly-wrapped, heavy-duty spiritual classics.

Of the many works cited in the many lists contained in these messages, there has never been any book listed that would be considered by any religion to be *a scripture*. And this is telling.

Not that scripture is the only sort of book worth reading, of course.
But the absence of scripture suggests how these people read.

In this busy, workaday world, people have become masters at
packing a broad variety of necessary activities and interests into
their lives. They work; have families, pets, political interests; go
to health clubs, conventions, PTA meetings.

When these busy people sense an absence of spiritual fulfillment
in their lives, one typical response is the resolution to "get spiritual" in the same way that one resolves to, say, lose weight, or
build muscles, or get a promotion at work. To become fulfilled
by hard work.

The hard work of losing weight is to either forgo eating or to
exercise more, and success is measured by the scale. The work of
building muscles is to exercise, and success is measured by how
much one can lift, or how far one can jump, or how long or fast
one can run. The work of getting a promotion might mean coming in early, staying late, completing projects ahead of schedule,
and knowing all aspects of a job, and is measured by actually getting the promotion.

People who have this mental outline about how to get what they want have a tendency to consume books as a measurable part of their work-output toward their goal of "getting spiritual." And as they strive to be efficient workers, they read a book and a half between the airport and the plane, on some red-eye turnaround between San Diego and Toledo.

They may find contradictions between books, contradictions of both flavor and substance, which they seek to resolve by . . . reading even more books. Truth by plebiscite.

And when reading all of those books makes the goal of spiritual fulfillment seem even more elusive than it was before, makes one feel that one has gone down a blind alley, one may unfortunately conclude: *It must be that I have not been working hard enough! I am not yet worthy!*

And thus they redouble their efforts, which means redoubling the ferocity of their reading.

Until they are distended and afloat, like spawned salmon.

✳ Getting Spiritual

NOW, WHAT CAN BE done about all of this?

First, I try to point out to them the way that scripture is read, and the way that they read. And talk about that a little. And then I tell them that they have a self-imposed timeline for "getting spiritual," which is completely out of whack with the pattern that unfolds the spirit. And I talk about that a bit. And then I tell them that half of their problem is that they have no particularly good idea about what spirituality is, and therefore don't know which way to head, and wouldn't know it even if they got there, which is not a great strategy for a traveler.

In regard to reading, I tell them about how Catholics read scripture during mass.

During the Catholic mass, the lector reads a few paragraphs from the Old and New Testaments, which is followed by the reading of the gospel by the priest. This reading then forms the basis of his homily, or sermon. The reading occurs in a place symbolic of God's presence and takes only a couple of minutes. The priest then develops the themes sounded by the reading, a verbal meditation upon scripture. In general, this homily notes a series of connections or relationships between aspects of the scriptural stories; then makes a series of connections between these noted aspects and the larger Faith. Starting at the particular, the homily then broadens itself into a wider view of spiritual wisdom.

This public process is common to many religions beyond Christianity; and contains an analogy for how one goes about reading spiritually, as an encompassing process of reading, meditation, and reflection; yielding a broader and more robust understanding of things of significance.

✳ The Art of Spiritual Reading

THE BENEDICTINES are a Catholic monastic order that practices a manner of reading known as *lectio divina*.

If I have any recall of public school Latin, *lectio divina* means "divine reading."

Let me quote Father Luke Dysinger, OSB, who has been formally instructed in this ancient art:

The art of lectio divina *begins with cultivating the ability to listen deeply, to hear "with the ear of our hearts" as St. Benedict encourages us in the Prologue to the Rule. . . . We should allow ourselves to become women and men who are able to listen for the still, small voice of God (I Kings 19:12); the "faint murmuring sound" which is God's word for us, God's voice touching our hearts . . . In order to hear someone speaking softly we must learn to be silent. We must learn to love silence. If we are constantly speaking or if we are surrounded with noise, we cannot hear gentle sounds. The practice of* lectio divina, *therefore, requires that we first quiet down in order to hear God's word to us. This is the first step of* lectio divina, *appropriately called* lectio—reading.*

The reading or listening which is the first step in lectio divina *is very different from the speed reading which modern Christians apply to newspapers, books and even to the Bible.* Lectio *is reverential listening; listening both in a spirit of silence and of awe. We are listening for the still, small voice of God that will speak to us personally—not loudly, but intimately. In* lectio *we read slowly, attentively, gently listening to hear a word or phrase that is God's word for us this day.*

Once we have found a word or a passage in the Scriptures which speaks to us in a personal way, we must take it in and "ruminate" on it. The image of the ruminant animal quietly chewing its cud was used in antiquity as a symbol of the Christian pondering the Word of God. Christians have always seen a scriptural invitation to lectio divina *in the example of the Virgin Mary "pondering in her heart" what she saw and heard of Christ (Luke 2:19). For us today these images are a reminder that we must take in the word—that is, memorize it— and while gently repeating it to ourselves, allow it to interact with our thoughts, our hopes, our memories, our desires. This is the second step or stage in* lectio divina*—meditation. Through meditation we allow God's word to become His word for us, a word that touches us and affects us at our deepest levels.*

The third step in lectio divina *is* oratio*—prayer: prayer understood both as dialogue with God, that is, as loving conversation with the One who has invited us into His embrace; and as consecration, prayer as the priestly offering to God of parts of ourselves that we have not previously believed God wants. In this consecration-prayer we allow the word that we have taken in and on which we are pondering to touch and change our deepest selves.*

Finally, we simply rest in the presence of the One who has used His word as a means of inviting us to accept His transforming embrace. No one who has ever been in love needs to be reminded that there are moments in loving relationships when words are unnecessary. It is the same in our relationship with God. Wordless, quiet rest in the presence of the One Who loves us, has a name in the Christian tradition— contemplatio, *contemplation. Once again we practice silence, letting go of our own words; this time simply enjoying the experience of being in the presence of God.*

Nicely put, Father.

So this is how the Benedictines would recommend we go about reading spiritual materials. In the same way that Patanjali recommended that we achieve intuition about anything: via concentration, meditation, and contemplation.

And do the speed-readers who write to me do that? Read like the Benedictines? Of course not.

Has the absorptive capacity of humankind for spiritual materials increased since the time of Benedict? Since the time of Patanjali? All evidence says not. Perhaps it is far worse.

The speed-readers don't understand that it is the soul's response to what is read that counts. Not the act of reading. Not having words run off one like a winter rain runs off the compacted desert.

So I tell them to stop reading, for a while.

But most can't stop, I'm afraid.

They're too hooched-up on the roar of words.

✸ To Sit with Him Alone

I ALSO TELL THEM that "getting spiritual" is not something that you can knock off in a certain time frame, like setting out to redo the kitchen. It's not an accomplishment.

It is, rather, a doing. I tell them that we will, as people, grow spiritually over time, this growth proceeding beyond death toward an indefinite and distant horizon.

And what is it that they're trying to do between now and next March?

In regard to spirituality, I tell them that the only spirituality that I can imagine occurs increasingly in God's presence, and therefore it is important for them to perceive God's presence. That once they sense God's presence, God will lead them from there. And so they should work on perceiving Him.

And once they have, like Father Dysinger, perceived God's presence, they should make a regular habit of sitting with Him alone.

What bliss it is to sit with Him alone!

And lest you fear too much of a good thing, know that after one sits with our Father alone, after this . . .

You get to go out in the yard and play.

✳ The Presence of God

MANY PEOPLE, at some point, sense the presence of God. They sense the presence of God as they pray. Sense the presence of God within their personal crises. Sense God's presence in the spring rain, as the wind comes up . . .

The presence of God marks you. Inscribes a groove. And as you spend more and more time with God, the groove deepens, until it regularly follows a well-worn path. The God of the morning. The God of toil. The God of the late afternoon, on the patio. The God of the late news.

The presence of God creates a dialogue between the transitory and the Ultimate, and in the dynamic between these aspects, intense meaningfulness becomes possible. Richness in life is richness in meaning, and meaning is created in His presence. His presence takes you where He intends for you to go, to places you cannot imagine.

And if you have no sense of His presence, this is the first thing to work on.

If you look at the monastic orders, this is the First Attainment.

There are some people who have read many books about spiritual matters and who are somewhat cynical about their ability to sense God's presence. After all, they have spent hundreds of hours reading about spiritual matters. If direct experience of God's presence were possible, by God, they would have sensed it.

But let me say this: what they have spent hundreds of hours doing is learning about the history of Zen Buddhism, or ancient Israel, or the Arabic words for heart and love. Rather than staring God in the face.

We do anything to avoid staring God in the face. Any dodge. Especially any dodge that seems spiritual, but isn't; from which we can plausibly seem to pay attention to Him, but don't.

All the traditional spiritual practices have, as either a primary or a secondary goal, the increased awareness of God. When one prays, the heart brings God into the greatest fullness it can imagine, as The One to Whom Prayer Is Addressed. One of the benefits of long periods of prayer is to practice being before God, and having God before oneself.

The Benedictines, who spend their days in prayer, are more present to God, and God is far more present to them than to the average person, due to long practice. The benefits of this life are quite real.

✳ Right Living

WITHIN THE READING PRACTICES of the Benedictines, there exists a set of conditions that are necessary not only for spiritual reading but also for leading a spiritual life.

I should first point out that when I talk of those elements necessary for leading a spiritual life, I am referring to a certain sort of contemplative spiritual life, where one sees and has access to God through contemplation. This is not the only spiritual life. There are, as we have discussed, a large number of active approaches that enable people to know and serve God, which are nonetheless not the subject of my discussion.

So what does it take to lead the life of a monk, the life of a Sufi, the life of an artist, a poet, a lover? What does it take to evince the level of contemplation needed by each of these persons to succeed?

Well, the life I describe does have certain prerequisites. And not everyone is equally suited to meet these prerequisites, or has the conditions in place to nurture this life if it arises. It being a somewhat temperamental flower, after all, and flourishing only under certain climates and conditions.

What are these conditions?

The first, I suppose, is something that I might call Right Living, although I mean something different by this term than what was meant by the Buddha, if you are familiar with Buddhism.

The Buddha called Right Living the livelihood that is morally and ethically sound. Right Living in Buddhism means making a living, or having a profession, that benefits the world, or is useful to its salvation; and not by doing something evil or morally suspect.

That is not what I mean by Right Living, although the Buddha's version of it is, of course, not a bad idea at all.

What I mean by Right Living is the art of arranging one's affairs so *that they are not all jammed together.*

It's to live a life that has a certain space within it. And where one has the chance to deal fully with each of the elements in it; and to appreciate the significance of each of its elements, a little, before moving on.

It is to live with a sense that one is walking down one's life, and is not being impelled down it as if on some kind of bobsled ride.

It is very difficult to progress on the contemplative life when one is hurtling through it.

And so if one aspires to the spiritual life that I describe, and yet one finds that one is hurtling through life, that hurtling is the first thing to fix, if one is serious about this path.

And like all important things, fixing a hurtling life is a difficult thing to do.

We sometimes get in a mode where the people in our lives become functions . . . our employees or bosses, our customers or students, plumbers or teachers, dispensers or demanders of cash . . . and it is easier to jam functions together in a busy life than it is to jam genuine human interaction together. In an overly full life, one tends to lop off those aspects of other people as people, as embodied souls, if you will, in order to enable everything to be crammed in.

The life I describe demands focus, to some degree, on other people as people, and not simply on their functions.

So to live rightly, in my sense, requires living in such a way that the elements in one's life have sufficient space, in both a psychological and a time sense, to be able to manifest their possibilities.

One might note that the way the Benedictines read, which is a slow and prayerful pondering of the words, is one that allows the words to have the psychological space, and the space in time, for certain spiritual possibilities to manifest themselves.

It is the same manner in which one gets value out of poetry.

Gets value out of a great painting.

Or children, parents, a spouse.

✳ What to Make of Religious Scripture

FOR ONE TO TRULY BENEFIT from reading a spiritual work, I would suggest that one read it as scripture is read. The question might then arise as to what is one to make of all those books of religious scripture?

All religions seem to congregate around a book. The Pentateuch, the New Testament, the Qur'an, the Vedas, the Sutras. Each of these books acts as a focus for a given community and as such, acts as a permanent touchstone that binds members of that community across time.

What are to be made of all these books?

I've read from them all, and how inspiring each of them is!

My goodness, what depths are there! What joy there is in a slow wander through any of them! What revelation! How worthy of emulation!

The spiritual excellence of each of them is intoxicating. Palpable.

And yet, I believe them all to be inspired works, not dictated works.

Being inspired, there are many layers and facets to each of them that reward our attention and our contemplation. Each of them has layers of surprise and wonder that cannot be exhausted.

Being inspired, there is an Otherworldly quality to scripture that cannot be denied. But though inspired, I believe that they were written, as all writing is written, by people who chose the next word to be written, and along the way edited the text if it did not sound quite right. (If God be in it, it was in the sound that did, or did not sound quite right.)

Though having a quality of Otherness, I do not believe that

scripture was written by God, at least in the way that most people mean it. The various scriptures are each culture's best approximation of the Ultimate, and that is why all scriptures do not agree, in total, on the finer points. The Ultimate of the Muslim is somewhat offset to the Ultimate of the Christian, which is somewhat offset to the Ultimate of the Jew.

It's not that one of them is right; it's that all of them are off, a little. All maintain a certain inflection, if you will. There being no completely authentic accent.

Each to a greater or lesser extent bears some mark of the person or culture that acted as intermediary to the Ultimate in the creation of the written work.

This tendency even exists within the same tradition. This is why, for example, the four canonic gospels of the New Testament differ, slightly, although they recount the same set of events. The gospels of Matthew, Mark, Luke, and John all feel a little different. Within Christianity, we have several formally approved perspectives, and yet the multiplicity of perspectives troubles us very little.

Different Christian persons, based on their inner lights, react more positively or negatively to one or more of these versions of the life of Jesus. For example, Christian evangelicals seem to like the gospel of John, if the signs at the baseball parks are any indication.

I, personally, am partial to the gospel of Matthew, and am sympathetic to Thomas, a non-canonic gospel. But the point I wish to make is that the Jesus of Matthew feels somewhat different than the Jesus of John. They're off a little. And that's OK. Looking at two separate images, slightly off, allows one to see things in 3-D. Similarly, the gospels of Matthew and John, being slightly off, allow one to see Christ in 3-D.

* * *

One might even consider the Trinity to be a formal invitation to mind-poise; God providing His own triangulation directions, as it were.

* * *

I mentioned earlier that of those three people whom I've met over the past thirty years who have had an experience like my own, there was a great (and should I say even a supernatural?) understanding between us.

Yet there were also subtle, but not inconsequential differences in our points of view, and also variations in tone in our understandings of the Other.

Although this example of my three friends and I does not constitute a meeting of Moses, Jesus, Mohammed, and the Buddha, it does, perhaps, suggest the reason we find a natural pattern of variation even among the greatest spiritual exemplars known to humankind.

All of these exemplars have a common view of the Ultimate, within the confines of their individuality. Their view of the Ultimate reflects the same basic vision, the experience of the same or a similar wholeness. Because of this, I believe that a meeting of these exemplars would find them to be in great and joyous accord.

The problem is primarily with their followers, who delight exclusively in their own prophets, messiahs, and teachers, while belittling all others. Who delight in their own scripture, while calling the scripture of others errors, or worse.

✵ Scripture Is Part of God's Providence

CLEARLY SCRIPTURE IS PART of God's providence, a gift to us all.

Although we all have the capacity within us to experience a direct mystical knowledge of God, the great majority of us are better suited to the active, rather than the contemplative, life.

Not everyone is a born mystic, nor should they be. There are as many ways to approach God as there are people, and mystical knowledge of God is but one way.

Scripture bridges the gap between active and contemplative lives, speaking to people in both realms about matters of great profundity. As such, scripture should never be treated lightly.

And of course, scripture should never be the provocation for the trading of blows. God gives us scripture to enlighten our hearts, after all, and not to make us more stiff-necked and self-righteous.

We're pretty stiff-necked and self-righteous already; and we need no further encouragement from the Almighty in this regard.

⤛ 7 ⤜

Fare Forward, Travelers!

✸ A Reconciled Journey

I SUPPOSE I SHOULD FIRST reconcile, to some degree, my own spiritual journey.

I have now discussed (at several points) that period of time, after my first experience, when I felt overwhelmed by God's continued presence.

As I age, I find that I am at peace just to be in the presence of those I love. My wife and I are approaching being an old married couple, just as God and I are. In much the same way as my wife and I have accommodated ourselves to each other, God and I have also accommodated ourselves to each other—me out of necessity, and He out of mercy.

Just as my wife and I have accommodated ourselves to each other.

Me of necessity, she out of mercy.

My heart can bear more now. When I stare God in the face, my joy rises. I no longer feel threatened by His overwhelming nature. Although I am still overmastered by God's presence, I am not fearful of Him. Rather, I am overmastered by joy in Him.

❊ A Condition Costing Not Less Than Everything

THE OVERWHELMING PRESENCE of God, early on, precipitated in me bouts of a particular spiritual anguish, an anguish about what my final outcome would be? Would I continue to be evermore myself? Or would my self become lost as I was poured back into God?

I was balanced between the desire to be folded into God and the desire to remain separate from God, and these twin desires were like a bone caught in my throat, which I could neither swallow nor bring back up.

When I had experienced myself as light, light upon light, in the light of God, it was an absolutely simple state, a state that knew of no before or after. Consciousness beyond form.

Was this state our human destiny?

What about those aspects of us that can be understood only when formed? Would those things go away? The knowledge and memory of all the people who were and are dear to us, and those places special and familiar, past and present?

T. S. Eliot and I share the same fear of loss. What happens to our memories? Are our memories lost? Is the structure of what makes us real destroyed in the Real?

Perhaps I should let him speak:

> *Through the unknown, remembered gate*
> *When the last of earth left to discover*
> *Is that which was the beginning;*
> *The voice of the hidden waterfall*

And the children in the apple-tree
Not known, because not looked for
But heard, half-heard, in the stillness
Between two waves of the sea.
Quick now, here, now, always—
A condition of complete simplicity
(Costing not less than everything)
And all shall be well . . .

My concern, at least years ago. A condition costing not less than everything.

❋ A Death in the Light

MY INTERNAL DEBATE on this point proceeded on spiritual, practical, and existential grounds.

If one turns one's attention to the larger universe, there is no hard evidence of life, sentient or otherwise, other than what's now on the face of this planet. Those SETI listening posts are still coming up empty; which, after all these years, rather surprises me.

I'd have figured that we'd be watching reruns of some alien *I Love Lucy* by now, and yet after decades of search, the sky is still quiet.

Almost alarmingly quiet.

This suggests to me that sentient, intelligent life, at least as we know it, is rather uncommon in the larger material universe.

Looking toward the night sky, we see light from stars that have been traveling toward us for millions, even billions, of years. Looking around us at our own world, we find our reality composed of atoms that have endured, in God, through billions and billions of years.

If God would accord enduring permanence to such simplicities as matter and light, shouldn't we expect that our personhood, which seems to come at such a premium to the universe, should survive? Wouldn't it be strange that He would create a survival stratagem for helium for the eons, but not for us?

To do so would seem, well, out of character.

It would also be an uninteresting choice for Him to make, and He is never, ever uninteresting.

He's a practical sort. The universe exists because it has a utility. It seems impractical that He would go to all that work to make people, just to have their final destiny be blackness and dust. If He wanted blackness and dust, He could have as easily made blackness and dust, and saved Himself the trip.

Since my experience of God, I've never had any fear that I will be unconscious and gone after death. No fear of being blackness and dust.

The death I have feared is a death in the Light.

✳ There Are Worse Things

I REMEMBER DISCUSSING THIS with my theology professor, the former Trappist, the first person I met who had had an experience like mine. He is a fine, gentle man, within whom I can see God, literally.

Back in that first year after my experience, I told him of my fear of becoming eternally effaced in God.

That upon death, I would be poured back into God, Light though He be, and that frightened me.

When I told my theology professor this, he said, softly, "Well, there are a lot worse fates than becoming part of God, I think."

❦ Embarrassingly Simple

YOU SEE, MY PROFESSOR had by that time submitted himself to God, and I had not. I had not yet come to the recognition, with my whole being, that God was more important than myself.

When you write it down, it seems completely sensible. Almost embarrassingly simple.

But that's not how most of us feel. We occupy ourselves in the belief that our God is our God, with the emphasis on *our. We* are still at the center.

Much of religious fundamentalism betrays this same egocentricity. Our God is *our* God, by God!

But, in fact, the thing that truly separates human beings is not Christian/Muslim/Jew or Hindu/Buddhist doctrine, but the degree of surrender to the Ultimate achieved by each person within each religion. The proud of each tradition are like the proud of any tradition; those who submit are like all who submit.

It's not the doctrine, but the spiritual character of the respondent that determines the outcome. This is the operation of spiritual law. It is not some silly test, but base reality.

Before one submits to God, one's perspective is essentially egocentric. My God is *my* God. God belongs to me. I do not belong to God.

To move away from this damaging, fundamentalist state (just look around the world to see how damaging!), one must submit to God. He is first. And when He is first, one is no longer in this center space.

✳ Submission

IT TOOK ME MANY YEARS not only to intellectually recognize but also to emotionally accept a state of submission to God. In that submission, there was a full recognition that whether or not I would continue into eternity was entirely up to Him. That He would know best, and whatever decision He made would be the right one.

And that that was OK.

This submission occurred during deep prayer and was enormously cathartic. I went away for a moment, was no longer me, and then came back again. The going out of existence, and then the coming back into existence.

And in the going out of existence, my concerns and fears had no longer anything to cling to and were washed away.

And in the coming back, I experienced a sort of ratification. I felt myself to be ratified by God.

What a vote of confidence!

I learned that, as unlikely as it may sound, one may personally exist, and then . . . not exist, without the concern that either state is final.

❦ The Antipodal Nature of Man

SOME YEARS LATER, I attended a lecture by Pir Vilayat Khan, the leader of a large and geographically diverse Sufi group, who spoke in a passing manner about the *antipodal nature of man*.

(Vilayat died in 2004 at the age of eighty-seven. He is quite a good old fellow, recently refreshed.)

Now, an *antipodal nature*, my dictionary informs me, is one that has an "exact opposite or contrary" nature. At some point in Vilayat's discussion of the antipodal nature of man, the penny dropped for me. Perhaps even more like a quarter, given the hearty plink in the bucket.

I understood then that most people tend to live in their daily existence, and that they experience life almost exclusively from that pole which embodies their individuality. People understand themselves to be John or Mary Smith, and live the life of John or Mary Smith. Relatively few people have mystical experiences, whereby it is revealed to them that they are part of a larger Reality. During these experiences, they are no longer as they were: no longer John or Mary Smith; but someone Other.

It's easy to think of the experience of God, and the realization that one is embedded in God, as the Ultimate Experience. And at some level, it is ultimate. At least it is the farthest one can go, down a particular pole. There is, after all, nothing simpler than Absolute Simplicity, no bliss greater than Absolute Bliss.

But it is not, as I have come to believe, ultimate in the sense that such simplicity, whether simplicity of blackness or the light, is our destiny.

It isn't our destiny, I don't believe. It's just one pole of our being.

Take a bar magnet, for example. One end of a bar magnet is the north pole, and the other end is the south. Cut the bar magnet in two, and each of the resulting pieces will still have a north and a south pole.

Both directions are deeply woven into the one thing.

Kind of like a photon is both a particle and a wave. The particle as an individuality, the wave as a larger phenomenon.

So you see, my anguish was misplaced in my search to discover whether my destiny was to be forever myself or forever God.

Having sought a too-simple solution, I had been caught on the horns of a dilemma that did not truly exist.

For God is still there, even when we have little thought of Him.

And we are still there, even when conscious of little other than God.

❋ A Chautauqua on Tree Climbing

A POEM! Time for a poem!

In late August when the air has blued
itself to dust, that tree on the low
hill, behind you, will offer you
a whispering, almost sexual
invitation: its languorous façade
belying a dim and unvarnished interior, the
deep-seated provenience of that
seemy underside of green.

If at the outset embarrassed by the
proximity of children, even dogs
all about their daily routines, please note
that you will be well-hidden in but
a few vertical feet.

To get inside your tree, you must jump, and
prying tug up your legs to the lowest limb,
and balance, and begin up,
a different branch for each hand
& foot, like the spider. Ascend until fear
exceeds exhilaration. Then rest.

Were you a smoker, you might smoke.
Contemplate the bottoms of birds, or perhaps
the sky that takes up that slack of leaves,
or perhaps still, below, the Ground
which now loiters, nonchalantly,
for your return. Both of you know it.

One way or another, you're
coming down.

✺ The Middle Point

AS WE PROGRESS to the middle-point, that place between the poles, we find it is the center of the dialogue that goes on between ourselves and God.

Not ourselves, not wholly God, but that middle-point, where we have availability to both ourselves and God. Where we have made room for Him.

To drink from that wide river created by our open-ended dialogue with Him, a dialogue about all manner of subjects.

And when the dialogue pauses, to have a simple, quiet joy in His presence.

✸ The Spiritual Versus the Holy

GOD'S PRESENCE HAS AN EFFECT on us and draws us inexplicably into a relationship with Him. This relationship, if sufficiently deep, is sometimes known as holiness.

In the West, our notion of what it is to be spiritual is often bound up with our notion of what it is to be holy.

To be holy is to experience ourselves as being embedded in God. To sense in ourselves that Otherness, that Otherworldly fragrance, which proximity to God gives.

This presence of Otherness as part of our being is also a significant part of what it is to be spiritual. But spirituality is a somewhat broader concept than simple holiness, although the path to holiness is certainly not simple, if recent census figures are to be believed.

In the East, the notion of spirituality is more complicated than that of sheer holiness. If one examines the literature of Zen Buddhism, for example, one finds a mass of stories and anecdotes about the interactions of realized and unrealized persons, with the unrealized persons acting as straight-men and woman in certain spiritual jokes.

Less common are those stories and anecdotes that relate the interactions of realized persons. In some of these stories, the straight-man is the less realized of the two. Often the difference between them is that the less realized has the "stink of enlightenment" or a "preference for transcendence." The more realized is not the one who sits for hours in meditation, but rather the one who takes a jug of wine and heads to the festival in the village.

Similarly, in Sufism, the ultimate goal of the person is not to become holy, but to become complete. It is hard to underestimate the importance, within Sufism, of the concept of *insan il kamil*, the Completed Person.

In the spirituality described by both Zen and Sufism, there is first the long road that leads to the discovery of the transcendent: the journey to become realized. Because of the difficulty of this first leg of the journey, the second leg receives less attention: the making of one's way back to the world.

The ultimate goal is to fully experience that spectrum of oneself that has union in God, while also having the ability to take individual action within the world.

To become fully at peace with one's existence, and also in the absence of one's existence.

✳ A Fish Story

ONE MIGHT REASONABLY ASK what my purpose was in writing this book. Is it a spiritual fish story of sorts? About the Big One who almost got away?

Well, yeah, kind of.

Although I hope that I also had a better reason to write it than just that.

I hope that the book is chockablock with helpful insights and useful tidbits. I hope.

Useful insights into the nature of the heart; about how to align it with the mind; and about the journey into God's presence, and the growth that may be found there.

And may be of some use to the traveler, as he or she hikes a difficult path.

✸ A Difficult Path

WHY SUCH a difficult path?

Well, it is hard enough, even in the physical world, to accumulate enough wealth to fund one's needs and desires.

Isn't it?

Hard to gather the wealth necessary to be able to afford the lifestyle that one deserves. We all, of course, being very highly deserving of a high lifestyle.

And it is hard parting with our money, even when it is to secure the lifestyle that we deserve.

Money being money; and greed, well . . . greed being that pandemic.

So harder still is it to part with pieces of ourselves, as we travel along the spiritual path.

For you see, we are our own currency.

✸ Take-Away

THROUGHOUT THIS BOOK, I've talked about a number of basic points.

First, how God is underneath our experience. Second, how the human person can access what is underneath the physical world by using the poetic faculty, the heart. And third, how an enlightened life is created in that space between human nature and God's presence.

In regard to God underneath our experience, let me say that the universe had a beginning, but it was not the Creation.

Creation is what is happening now. As you read this.

It's this that makes mysticism possible. That God is not separate from our reality, but rather is Reality, and is underneath our daily experience. Were God divorced from our reality, having simply set the wheels spinning eons ago, you would not be able to find Him. He is not a Ghost in the machine, but is both Ghost and Machine. Carefully study the Machine, and you may find the Ghost!

All that we understand as the phenomenal world is the instant creation of God, and all motion and apparent change happens within Him. And we, as part of Him, participate in the making of our Reality though the creative nature of our perceptions of the world and our actions within the world. So as children of God, we are allowed to participate, a little, in the production of the nature of things. Decorate our rooms, at it were. And potentially half-accidentally strangle one's pet, if the Middle East be considered.

When one understands that creation occurs at this very moment of our experience, it is easy to sense God's presence. It is as apparent as our being in the world. God no longer belongs to a field of action billions of years ago, with an infinite future, but is participating with us now. Is the Living God. Living now, with us. Us living now.

And as we succeed in sensing God's presence, the events of our days will teach us, and our dreams will teach us. Meaning is created in the matrix between God's presence and our own. The events of our own lives become our dialogue with God, and we grow in the spirit as our dialogue with God, and our lives, continues.

In the presence of God, one understands that the full weight of the spirit is continually and constantly available to each of us, modulated only by our ability to relate to it. One need not go off on a grand search to find the All, but one must search within oneself, within one's daily life and daily experience, to find and unveil the Real.

✻ The Overlay of Perspectives

THROUGHOUT THIS BOOK, I have stressed the importance of having many different windows upon reality, and overlaying these windows in order to cobble together a broader view of Reality, which is God's nature. The human experience of reality is a faceted thing. This faceting is due to our perceptual equipment; equipped, as it were, by the chakras, which break Reality into different perspectives; and also into manners of exploration as diverse as the arts, science, golf and religion.

God is not out to mislead us, but to inform us in every possible dimension of the head and heart; and these perspectives must be overlaid (because the edges do not match) to approximate the truth. Because the human experience of God has a faceted nature, and each facet is in its own, separate plane, it is impossible to connect up Reality as though it were a jig-saw puzzle. There is no clean edge between Science and Religion, for example. This is why the perspectives must be overlaid, rather than connected.

The study of religion in the absence of the study of science leads to errors in the study of religion. The study of science in absence of the study of the arts leads to errors in the study of science. The study of the arts in absence of the study of mathematics leads to error in the knowledge of the arts. One needs to know something about everything, in order to resolve, a little, the God of Everything.

❦ Going Forward

WHAT DO I HOPE you will take from this book?

Well, I hope that when you go outdoors in the spring, you will look at the world differently. That you will mindfully know your heart as you breathe in the spring air. And that you will notice the poetic faculty, the heart, in operation.

See? That's not hard.

That's fun.

Also, I would have you understand the spiritual process a bit better.

Spirituality is an apprenticeship of the heart, and God is the master.

As we becomes competent in the recognition and use of the heart, we begin to peer through the world, to a set of conditions that underlie the world.

It is the heart that knows God's presence, and once God's presence is found, our world changes. The world is seen as derivative of God, and we begin to discern the ways of God.

Being in God's presence makes certain demands of us. It demands, for example, that we grow. There is this great longing deep within us that desires to know God ever better, and makes our growth an imperative. And so we grow in response to God's command, and as a command of God, that growth is certain. Guaranteed.

And as we grow, we are ever better able to submerge ourselves in God. And to rejoice there.

In doing that, what we are will change. That change will be a movement toward spiritual maturity, as children of God. And as children of God, we will leave the world a better place, as the result of at least some of our actions in God.

On many occasions throughout this book, I've discussed the heart as the locus of spiritual perception; or the poetic faculty; or the faculty that penetrates the world.

When you see something of great beauty, note the operation of the heart.

When you discern something profoundly true, note the operation of the heart.

When you love, note that which underlies the heart. Note the heart's role in your hopes and joys.

And as you continue to take notice of your heart, you will become better able to use it consciously, in the same way that you consciously use your sense of vision when lining up a photograph. To consciously use the heart, you must bring it into mindfulness while it is in operation. Recognize its role when you are having a moment of epiphany.

It is the heart that will allow you to observe the patterns of things that underlie the world, and to find God there. So work, over the years, to find a deeper understanding of the heart, and what it is capable of.

The heart can be used as part of an overall orientation of sensitivity toward other people, or the world, or God. It can be used, along with the mind, when seeking specific revelation through the process of mind-poise. The heart can find and hold God. It is through the heart that God is beheld, and through which His presence is known.

Study the heart.

Reflect on God's presence. When we pray, we summon God's presence before us in supplication as He to Whom We Pray. Learn to recognize His same presence even when you are not praying.

Reflect on creation being this very moment of your experience. Know Him now.

And why is knowing God's presence so important?

Well, when you understand God's presence, your life becomes something like a play, and you and God are the audience of your life. Oh, your friends and family, coworkers and neighbors all share your life to some greater or lesser extent, but in regard to your life, it is only you and God who are fully invested in it.

When you and God have a dialogue through the medium of your life, even the smallest act takes on meaning. The request acceded to or denied, the opportunity pursued or abandoned, the moment of sudden generosity or greed, a small joy or sorrow . . . all these may yield some important lesson or be part of some larger experiment in the crucible of life.

And as this dialogue continues, the level of meaning that is evoked becomes progressively more subtle, connecting subjects and events that are widely diverse in both emphasis and time. I am not suggesting a more superstitious view of your life, but rather an increasing sensitivity toward revelation, a teasing of meaning out of the heretofore unobserved.

As this process continues over the years, it will serve as the engine of your spiritual growth, a growth that not only will deepen your understanding of yourself, God, and the world; but will also increase your capacity to live life fully, to live in ways that would have formerly been considered inexplicable.

All this from dwelling in God's presence. And better still . . .

When you are practiced in God's presence; when you are just hanging out with God as with an old friend, well, sometimes you may just wish to be in His presence, and to look Him in the face. Face Him without any thoughts, any words, with no agenda other than looking at Him. And find bliss there.

He's easy that way.

Notes and Further Reading

My source for those quotations taken from the New Testament is *The New Testament of the Jerusalem Bible*, Image Books edition, 1969, printed by special arrangement with Doubleday & Company, Inc.

Quotations from Wm Blake's *Marriage of Heaven and Hell* are taken from *English Romantic Writers*, edited by David Perkins, and published by Harcourt, Brace & World, Inc., 1967.

Passages taken from Rumi are the translation of Coleman Barks (with John Moyne) in *The Essential Rumi*, 1995.

Quotations from T.S. Eliot's *Four Quartets* are based on the Harvest Book edition, Harcourt, Brace & World, Inc. by special arrangement with Esme Valerie Eliot, 1971.

Ernest Wood's *Practical Yoga*, published by E. P. Dutton & Co., Inc., 1948, was the source of several cited quotations on the practice of mind-poise and Raja Yoga.

The attributes of the visuddha chakra was quoted from Ajit Mookerjee's excellent book, *Kundalini*, Destiny Books, Third Edition, 1986.

The lyrics quoted from John Hiatt's song *Little Head* are from the album of the same name, Capitol, 1997.

The lyrics quoted from George Harrison's song *Pisces Fish* are from his *Brainwashed* album, Dark Horse/Capitol, 2002.

The news item about Michael Persinger, God and the brain was reported by Michael Martin and Joe O'Connor, of ABC News, in 2002.

Paul Repp's translation of the Zen story *The Stone Mind* was quoted from *Zen Flesh, Zen Bones*, a Doubleday Anchor book, published by arrangement with the Charles E. Tuttle Company.

The discussion of *lectio divina* was drawn from *Accepting the Embrace of God: The Ancient Art of Lectio Divina* by Fr. Luke Dysinger O.S.B. This essay was found on the Saint Andrew's Abbey website, www.valyermo.com.

In Appreciation

Joseph Smith. Pat Ward. John Schmitt. Jim Wilson. Stephen Hall. Adam Singh. Ric Simpson. Chitra Rajyashree. Rich Reilly. My wife and kids. Humanity at large; at least some of them.

About the Author

William Widmer is a painter, poet, husband, father, corporate middle-manager, and gardener, who is the leader of a Western Sufi group.

Widmer's dedication to the truth began at the age of seventeen, when he had what may be termed "an enlightenment experience" that dissolved his old identity, and sent him skittering down a different path. The decades that followed were devoted to understanding and integrating the experience, and its aftermath.

For the past thirty years, Widmer has lived outside the same small, New England village where Robert Frost had spent some of his boyhood. It is also a town that Henry David Thoreau once declared to be: "a drab place, of no particular note."

Of course, that comment dated from prior to Frost's arrival. And Henry David probably never visited it in autumn, either.